get cooking

Sam Stern – and Susan Stern, who got him started

WALKER BOOKS
AND SUBSIDIARIES

LONDON · BOSTON · SYDNEY · AUCKLAND

Contents

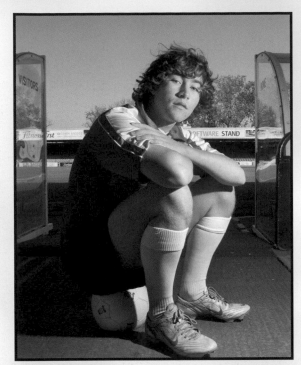

WELCOME TO MY THIRD BOOK. Get Cooking. How did it come about? OK I love a challenge. So when seven mates asked me to sort out some top tasting recipes based on their one favourite food I went for it.

It wasn't easy. Particularly as some of them went for whole food groups (thanks guys) instead of single ingredients. But no problem, I just got into the kitchen and got a bit creative. You'll see the book's got 8 chapters — one for each mate and their ingredient of choice. That's tomatoes from Jess, cheese from Henry, pasta from Ariyo, vegetables from Joe, meat from Andy, potatoes from Liv, sweet stuff from Verity. I kept the best for myself — chocolate. You'll meet all my mates later.

Why cook?

Hey, you're missing out if you don't do it. Every part of the process has got something cool going for it. First off — the shopping. Nope it doesn't grow in carriers. Food shopping means you get to visit some great markets, shops, delis, farm shops — even the supermarket. Do it. Get out there. Talk to the people who've grown the stuff or made it. You want to know as far as possible where your food has come from and how it's been produced. Keep it real. You want it to be good if you're going to swallow it. Cooking gives you power in loads of ways. It's a great way to be independent —

chucking some good stuff together when you're just in or before you go out. Getting yourself ready for when you escape from home to work, college, gap year, uni, whatever. Cooking the right stuff can prop you up (after a night out) sort you out (when you're feeling lousy or exams loom) turn you on (head straight for chocolate or pudding) give you the energy you need just to get you through the day or the party the game or another night of training. Then there's the ultimate pleasure of the cooking itself. The hands-on and senses stuff – the smell and sight of chocolate melting down, separating an egg, kneading dough, curing salmon, making puffy Yorkshires, putting together a whole roast dinner, watching a mess of a pudding mix transform itself through the cooking into something magnificent and so appetizing.

Cooking gets you into politics too. Over the last year there's been loads of debate about food, organic vs non-organic, fast food vs slower food (no contest) growing your own food (do it – in tyres, flower gardens, windowboxes – even windowsills need filling) and food miles (read labels – get local if you can as it should be fresher and better but check it out). Cooking's the key to everything. It takes you beyond the plate to a great way of living.

Finally the best bit. Feeding other people for everyday meals, parties, gatherings. It's all about good times. Everyone helping out in the kitchen then sitting around eating together and having a good laugh. Cooking for mates and family is the greatest pleasure (and well impressive).
So over to you.

Enjoy and Get Cooking.

PS Check out the website on www.samstern.co.uk for regular cooking updates, a blog and the latest hot food news.

Tomatoes

Jess has great taste and likes to take care of herself so no surprise she went for tomatoes. They're healthy (eyes, skin, immune system fixers. Who needs make-up?) Stylish. Versatile. Perfect to photograph. Slice 'em up with a bit of shallot or herbs and a sharp dressing or cook 'em up for my salsa, bakes, soup, homestyle ketchup. Support the main event in awesome meat dishes (lush tomato sauce with griddled steak or my style chicken parmigiana). Use sundried in a marvellous burger. Skin and chop 'em small for an impressive retro cocktail or tuna & mash dressed up in tomato. Blitz 'em raw for dipping your dough balls. Winter tomatoes can be inferior bad boys. OK they look cool, but it's all skin-deep. Use canned instead (Italian make or best you can) for a great margherita-style tart and deeply flavoured sauces. Buying fresh? Sniff.

They want to smell peppery. Grow a load of cherry tomatoes on your windowsill (late July– August). Larger varieties work in a flower bed, growbag, camerabag, handbag…

Tomato, Squash & Parma Ham Salad

For 4

1 butternut squash
Olive oil for roasting
Sprinkle of crushed chilli
  flakes
1/2 tsp ground cumin
Sea salt and pepper
1 ciabatta or focaccia
  loaf, cubed
8–12 slices Parma or
  other thin ham
16–20 cherry tomatoes
  (some red, some
  yellow's nice)
Rocket or spinach leaves
Parmesan shavings or curls
Olive oil and balsamic
  vinegar for drizzling

variation

VEGETARIAN
Sub ham and Parmesan
with chunks of smoked
cheese, avocado and
sliced red onion.

This is well nice. Cherry tomatoes create bursts of flavour that work brilliantly with these other tastes and textures. Be artistic with your assembly. Missing an ingredient? Experiment with substitutes.

Method

1. Preheat oven to 200°C/400°F/gas 6.
2. **Squash:** Wash and dry. Lay it flat on a board. Slice the two ends off. Hold firmly and cut in two lengthways down the centre. Remove seeds with a spoon. Discard.
3. Cut squash into bite-sized bits. Slap on an oiled roasting tin or baking tray. Drizzle and coat with olive oil. Sprinkle with chilli, cumin, sea salt and pepper. Bake for 20 minutes plus till soft and just browning (could take longer).
4. **Croutons:** Meantime roll bread cubes in a bit of oil and salt. Cook on a baking tray for 5 minutes plus, till crisp and golden.
5. **Assemble:** Drape ham over plates. Slap squash in between with cherry tomatoes, rocket or spinach. Scatter croutons and curls or shavings of Parmesan over the lot. Drizzle with a bit of olive oil and/or balsamic or favourite dressing.

Tomato Chilli Salsa & Dough Balls

Dunk your own dough balls into this brilliant tomato chilli salsa for a popular spicy hit. Stuffed or plain, they're perfect for parties. Knock out a few when next making pizza.

Method

1. Dough: Make pizza dough (pg 34) but at STEP 1 add garlic and rosemary. Follow recipe until the end of STEP 3.

2. Preheat oven to 220°C/425°F/gas 7. Lightly grease 2 baking trays.

3. Slap risen dough onto a lightly floured board. Knead for 2 minutes.

4. Plain balls: Break bits off. Roll into smooth, neat walnut-sized balls.

Stuffed balls: Shape each bit into a smooth, flat circle. Stick an olive or cheese chunk in the middle. Draw dough up and round to cover it. Pinch the ends firmly together. A bit of water may help to seal.

5. Sit balls apart on trays, seam down. Brush with milk or beaten egg. Bake for 15 minutes or till cooked and golden. Split a bit? No problem!

6. Salsa: Chuck ingredients in blender or processor. Blitz till smooth. Sieve into a pan. Heat gently (don't boil). Taste and adjust seasoning.

7. Dunk hot (or cold) balls into warm salsa.

Makes 20–30 balls
Pizza dough (pg 34)
3 cloves garlic, finely chopped
1–2 sprigs rosemary, finely chopped
Beaten egg or milk for brushing

Fillings
Pitted olives
Mozzarella, cubed

Salsa
450 g/1 lb tomatoes, chopped
1 small onion, peeled and halved
2 cloves garlic, peeled
2 red chillies, de-seeded and finely chopped
1 tsp caster sugar
Salt and black pepper
Juice of 1 lime
2 tbsps olive oil

why not?
Dunk into:
Salsa verde (pg 80)
Garlic butter (pg 98)
Yogurt & dill

Tomato & Mozzarella Bruschetta

For 2
2 slices good white bread
   or focaccia
A little olive oil
110 g/4 oz Mozzarella
2–3 tomatoes
1 clove garlic
Salt and pepper

Dressing
1 tsp olive oil
1 tsp red wine vinegar
   or lemon juice

variations
CHEESE & HAM
Lay a slice of ham
under Mozzarella
before baking.
MORE TOMATO
Rub half a whole tomato
over crisped bread
at the end of STEP 5.

I make this all the time when I'm in from school or fancy something light but good. Bits of warm tomato lift the taste of the cheese on the crisp bread base. It may be simple, but it's pretty lovely.

Method
1. Preheat oven to 200°C/400°F/gas 6.
2. Sit the bread on a baking tray. Drizzle with a little olive oil. Bake till just crisp (5–10 minutes).
3. Meantime slice the Mozzarella thinly (5 mm/¼ in).
4. Chop tomatoes into small cubes.
5. Remove bread from the oven. Rub a cut clove of garlic over it.
6. Lay Mozzarella over the breads to cover. Stick just a few bits of tomato on top with a few drops of olive oil.
7. Bake till cheese is just softening – could be as little as 3–5 minutes. Remove just before it melts.
8. Eat as is or slap a few more bits of tomato on top. You can sit more bits of tomato on the side with spinach, lettuce or rocket and dressing.

Scarlet Couscous & Veggie Skewers

Liven up your couscous with tomato juice for this cool, light eat. OK, it sounds weird but you'll get a bit of a fizz and a brilliant colour to set off your skewers. Perfect if you've got a few mates round or you're treating family.

Method

1. Tip tomato juice, oil, lemon juice, water and garlic into a bowl.

2. Pour couscous into a larger bowl. Tip the liquid into it. Mix well. Cover with a cloth. Leave for 1 hour or longer.

3. Slap raisins into a small bowl. Cover with 2–3 tablespoons boiling water and the same of tomato juice.

4. Chop tomatoes into small cubes (skin and deseed if you want to – see pg 14). Dice the cucumber, pepper and onion.

5. Test couscous. Should be soft. Stir in a tablespoon of hot water if not.

6. Season with salt and pepper. Stir in the tomatoes, cucumber, pepper, onion and herbs. Drain the raisins. Chuck them in. Pile onto a plate. Chill for later or heat the grill and cook the veggies.

7. Thread tomatoes, onion, mushrooms and courgettes onto metal skewers or wooden ones presoaked in cold water for 20 minutes.

8. Beat the oil and vinegar together. Drizzle over the veg.

9. Grill. Turn regularly till browned and just tender. Serve with couscous.

For 3–4

150 ml/5 fl oz tomato juice, plus extra for marinade
50 ml/2 fl oz olive oil
Juice of 1½ lemons
30 ml/1 fl oz boiling water
1 clove garlic, crushed
175 g/6 oz couscous
25 g/1 oz raisins
2 large or 3 medium tomatoes
15 cm/6 in piece cucumber
1 red pepper, de-seeded
1 small red onion
Salt and black pepper
1 bunch parsley
1 bunch mint

Veg skewers

225 g/8 oz cherry tomatoes
1 large red onion, chopped
225 g/8 oz button mushrooms
350 g/12 oz courgettes, sliced
2 tbsps olive oil
2 tbsps balsamic vinegar

Eat with:

Lamb koftas (pg 90)
Homestyle burgers (pg 88)
Griddled Halloumi

Retro Tomato & Prawn Cocktail

For 4
2 tomatoes
225 g/8 oz best North
   Atlantic peeled prawns
Little gem lettuce
Dressing
1 tbsp tomato ketchup
   (pg 139)
3 tbsps Greek yogurt
   or crème fraîche
3 tbsps mayo
Juice of 1 lemon
1 small clove garlic, crushed
Few drops of Tabasco,
   horseradish or wasabi
   sauce
Salt
Cayenne pepper

Eat with: Slices of brown
bread and butter.

---

variations
AVOCADO
Chop fresh avocado
into the mix and sit
it on bread for an
open sandwich.
TORTILLA
Wrap it up in a
soft tortilla.

Lovely and light with a bit of a bite. Prawns get a cool double tomato dose. Jess piles this one high for a romantic starter. PS Prawns are so good for you…

Method
1. Skinning: Stick tomatoes into a large heatproof bowl. Pour boiling water over them. Leave for 2 minutes. Drain into a colander.
2. Peel the skins off. Chop tomatoes into quarters. Remove seeds with a teaspoon. Cut remaining flesh into tiny pieces.
3. Dressing: Mix all dressing ingredients well. Taste and adjust the balance of flavours.
4. Piling: Slap a bit of diced tomato on a plate or into the base of a short tumbler or glass. Cover with a bit of shredded lettuce.
5. Mix 2/3 of the dressing into the prawns and remaining diced tomato. Sit this on top of the lettuce. Top with remaining dressing.

Lovely Tomato & Garlic Soup

Roast your tomatoes for this awesome soup and you'll get the best out of them. Blasting them with heat and garlic maximizes their flavour. Tomatoes are health gods.

Method

1. Preheat oven to 220°C/425°F/gas 7.

2. Roast tomatoes: Sit them on a baking tray. Drizzle with olive oil. Roast for 20–25 minutes or till their skins split.

3. Vegetable base: Meantime heat 2 tablespoons of olive oil in a large pan on low heat. Slap in onions, carrot and celery. Cook gently for 5–10 minutes till soft and sweating. Stir with a wooden spoon.

4. Garlic: Slice the very top off the whole garlic. Separate cloves. Sit them on the baking tray with roasting tomatoes. Drizzle with oil. Bake with tomatoes for a further 10–15 minutes till soft. Remove.

5. Soup: Smush the garlic out of its skin. Careful, it's hot. Tip tomatoes and garlic cloves in with the sweated vegetables. Add water, sugar, herbs and seasoning. Bring to the boil then reduce immediately. Cover and simmer for 30 minutes.

6. Remove from the heat. Cool for a bit then blitz in a blender till smooth. Reheat, taste and adjust seasoning.

For 4

900 g/2 lb ripe medium-sized tomatoes
3–4 tbsps olive oil
2 large onions, chopped
1 carrot, peeled and sliced
1 stick celery, sliced
1 head of garlic
600 ml/1 pint water
2 tsps caster sugar
2 tbsps parsley or coriander
Salt and black pepper

Eat with:

Good warm crusty bread
Croutons (pg 10)
Grated Parmesan
or Cheddar
A whirl of sour cream
Some basil leaves smashed
with a bit of balsamic
vinegar, salt and sugar

Chinese Ketchup Spare Ribs

For 4
1.35 kg/3 lbs meaty pork
  spare ribs
Marinade
3 tbsps tomato ketchup
  (pg 139)
3 tbsps soy sauce
3 tbsps rice wine
125 ml/4 fl oz hoisin sauce
2 tbsps caster sugar
4 cloves garlic, crushed
Piece of fresh ginger, peeled
  and roughly grated
1 red chilli, de-seeded and
  sliced, or 1 tbsp sweet
  chilli sauce

Why not make up a batch of homestyle ketchup to give this great Chinese spare rib recipe a healthy kick? It really lifts the marinade – the concentrated tomato taste does it. Great for main meals, barbies, Chinese-style banquets.

Method

1. Put the ribs into a large casserole dish with water to cover.

2. Bring to the boil. Reduce heat and simmer very gently for 15 minutes. Drain in a colander and allow to cool.

3. Meantime mix all the marinade ingredients. Pour into a large shallow dish which is big enough to hold the ribs.

4. Put the cold ribs into the marinade. Turn them to coat. Leave for the flavours to catch for a couple of hours or even overnight.

5. Preheat oven to 180°C/350°F/gas 4.

6. Lay the ribs out over a rimmed baking tray lined with foil. Brush with marinade. Bake for 20 minutes each side till tender and golden. Rest the meat somewhere warm for 5 minutes.

7. If you're making a complete meal, cook your rice and make a stir-fry 15 minutes before you eat. Serve ribs with rice, stir-fry and soy sauce.

Smart Margherita Tart

Pretty straightforward. Pretty delicious. It's a pizza kind of tomatoey tart. Using tinned tomatoes makes it an all-year-rounder. Brilliant for parties or general sharing. Team with a bunch of lovely salads.

Method

1. **Make pastry:** By hand or processor (pg 138).
2. Grease a 23 cm/9 in loose-based tart tin.
3. Roll pastry out lightly on a floured board. Make it big enough to fit the base plus sides of the tin.
4. **Line tin:** Ease one edge of the pastry off the board. Roll the pin underneath to the centre then use it to lift pastry up and over the tin. Let pastry down onto tin then roll pin away carefully. Mould pastry gently into the tin. Fill any gaps with extra pastry. Press tears together. Chill for 30 minutes.
5. **Filling:** Gently heat oil and butter in a large pan over a low heat. Add onion and garlic. Cook till soft, not coloured.
6. Slap in tomatoes, sugar, half the optional chopped anchovies (save anchovy oil for later) and purée. Boil. Reduce heat. Simmer for 20 minutes. Preheat oven to 200°C/400°F/gas 6.
7. Cool mixture slightly. Add eggs and half the herbs. Pour into tart.

8. Top with remaining whole anchovies, olives and herbs. Sprinkle with Parmesan and anchovy oil if using.
9. Bake for 30 minutes. Reduce heat to 180°C/350°F/gas 4. Cook for another 15 minutes or till crisp and set.

For 4–6
Pastry
See pg 138
Filling
2 tbsps olive oil
1/2 oz butter
1 medium–large onion, chopped
3 cloves garlic, peeled and crushed
2 x 400 g/14 oz cans chopped tomatoes
Pinch of sugar
1 x 50 g/2 oz tin anchovies, drained (optional)
2 tbsps tomato purée
3 eggs, beaten
Handful of basil or parsley, torn
Black olives
Parmesan for sprinkling

Eat with:
Green salad (pg 140)
Baked potatoes (pg 98)
Coleslaw (pg 141)
Orange salad (pg 140)

Makes 4

450 g/1 lb beef for mincing (rump's good) or quality steak mince

1 small onion, peeled and finely chopped

1 clove garlic, peeled and crushed

50 g/2 oz sundried tomatoes, chopped small

2 tsps tomato ketchup (pg 139)

$1/2$ tbsp horseradish sauce or a splash of Worcester sauce

1 tbsp chopped parsley

Salt and black pepper

Sunflower oil

Stacking

4 burger buns

Ketchup

Little gem lettuce, shredded

Fresh tomatoes, thinly sliced

Celery & Apple Salad

2 sticks celery, thinly sliced

1 small apple, thinly sliced

2 tbsps mayo

1 tbsp Greek yogurt or crème fraîche

1 tsp Dijon mustard

Drizzle of honey

Salt and pepper

---

why not?

Dry your own tomatoes. Slice tomatoes in two. Oven dry for 8–10 hours at 170°C/325°F/gas 3 sitting on a rack on a baking tray. Cherry tomatoes dry faster. Put into jars covered with olive oil.

Tangy Tomato Burgers & Salad

Slap flavour-packing sundried tomatoes into these cool burgers and you've got yourself an awesome dish. Make shedloads for gatherings and parties.

Method

1. Own mince: Cut beef into cubes. Blitz a few at a time in the processor or mincer till it looks like shop mince. Don't paste it.

2. Chuck own or good steak mince in a bowl with the other burger ingredients. Season. Fry a crumb in hot oil. Taste so you can judge it.

3. Shape firmly into 4 flattish burgers. If mix is flaky add a splash of beaten egg, ketchup or mayo to bind it. Chill for 30 mins or get cooking.

4. Preheat grill, griddle or frying pan. Cook for 3 minutes each side (turn with care) or till done as you like. Rest meat for 2 minutes.

5. Salad: Mix all salad ingredients together in a bowl.

6. Stack burgers as you like. Enjoy with loads of salad.

Baked Egg Stuffed Tomatoes

A good little snack to crack into when you've got mates round for brunch or to treat yourself any time. Getting the egg into the tomatoes can be a challenge, but enjoy yourself – it's worth it.

Method

1. Slice tops off the stem end of tomatoes. Using a teaspoon and sharp knife, hollow them out completely. Don't break the skins.
2. Season insides with salt, pepper and garlic. Sit them upside down for 10–20 mins to drain. Preheat oven to 200°C/400°F/gas 6.
3. Sit tomatoes on a greased baking tray.
Fill: Crack each egg in turn over a bowl, letting a bit of white spill out. Carefully slip the rest of the egg into a tomato.
4. Cover the top with Parmesan or make a mix of cream, tomato purée and Parmesan. Spoon that over.
5. Bake for 15 mins or till set as you like.
6. Sit on bits of toast or bread fried both sides in a bit of olive oil.

For 2
4 large tomatoes
Salt and pepper
2 cloves garlic, crushed
4 small–medium eggs
Parmesan, freshly grated
2 tbsps double cream or crème fraîche
2 tsps tomato purée (optional)
4 slices white bread
Olive oil

Eat with:
Lightly fried mushrooms
Crisp bacon

variation
MUSHROOMS
Try with deep cup mushrooms instead of tomatoes.

My Style Chicken Parmigiana

For 4
Classic tomato sauce (pg 21)
4 chicken breasts
Salt and pepper
1 garlic clove, crushed
4 slices Parma ham
150 g/5 oz ball Mozzarella
   or Fontina cheese, sliced
4 fresh basil leaves
   (optional)
Seasoned flour
2 eggs, beaten
50 g/2 oz white
   breadcrumbs
Olive oil
Butter

Eat with:
Chopped chicory &
watercress salad in my
mustard dressing (pg 140)

This isn't just about a classic tomato sauce. It's about a classic tomato sauce with the coolest chicken dish. The amount of flavour going on is totally ridiculous – as a tomato fan you've just got to make it.

Method

1. Make the tomato sauce (pg 21). Preheat oven to 220°C/425°F/gas 7.

2. If chicken breasts are very plump, lay a stretch of clingfilm out on a board. Slap a piece of chicken on top. Cover with clingfilm.

3. Bash the chicken to flatten it a bit using a rolling pin or the palm of your hand. Don't make it too thin as you need to stuff it.

4. Cut the chicken laterally across to create a pocket in the side.

5. Season with salt, pepper and garlic. Put in your ham, cheese and optional basil leaf. Press edges of chicken well to seal. Repeat.

6. Put your seasoned flour onto a large plate, beaten eggs on another. Spread the breadcrumbs on a third.

7. Heat the oil and butter in a large frying pan.

8. Dip the whole of each fillet into seasoned flour then egg then crumbs till covered. Fry for 2–3 minutes each side to seal.

9. Bake on a greased baking tray for 10–15 minutes. Test with a sharp knife to check that it is white all through and moist.

10. Reheat tomato sauce (blitz it up if you want). Slap round the chicken.

Aubergine Roll-ups in Lush Sauce

A classic Italian dish. Soft strips of aubergine get stuffed with melting cheese 'n' herbs, layered in full-on tomato sauce. Get on your mobile. Get some mates round.

Method

1. Sauce: Heat olive oil gently in a pan. Cook garlic and onion for 5 minutes or till soft, not coloured. Add tomatoes, sugar, salt and pepper.

2. Reduce heat. Simmer gently for 15–20 minutes. If it gets too thick, add a splash of water. Taste. Adjust seasoning. Add lemon juice.

3. Veg: Meantime slice each aubergine into 5–6 thin lengths.

4. Slap flour on a large plate. Season it. Slap eggs on another plate.

5. Tip a few glugs of oil into a large frying pan. Heat gently.

6. Meantime dip aubergine slices into flour then egg till coated. Increase heat. Fry for 1–2 minutes each side or till golden. Rest on kitchen paper. Cook remainder.

7. Preheat oven to 200°C/400°F/gas 6.

8. Spread a bit of tomato sauce in the base of a large, shallow ovenproof dish.

9. Roll: Sprinkle each aubergine slice with salt, pepper and Parmesan. Add a basil leaf and a teaspoon of grated Halloumi or small slice of Mozzarella. Roll the veg over its filling. Place seam down on tomato sauce. Repeat. Save half Mozzarella for topping.

10. Cover rolls with remaining sauce. Top with sliced Mozzarella, Parmesan and a drizzle of oil. Bake for 20 minutes or more till hot and bubbling.

For 4

Lush tomato sauce
4 tbsps good olive oil
1–2 cloves garlic, crushed
1 small onion, finely chopped
400 g/14 oz tin chopped tomatoes or plum tomatoes, drained
Pinch of sugar
Salt and pepper
Squeeze of lemon juice

Veg rolls
2 large firm shiny aubergines
3 tbsps flour
Salt and pepper
2 eggs, beaten
Olive oil for frying
3–4 tbsps freshly grated Parmesan
A bunch of fresh basil
110 g/4 oz Halloumi plus 225 g/9 oz Mozzarella, or 350 g/12 oz Mozzarella
Extra Parmesan and olive oil for topping

Eat with: Warm crusty bread and green salad (pg 140).

why not?

Fry 2 slices of aubergine till soft in a little garlicky olive oil. Season lightly. Lay between slices of focaccia or panini, with sliced Mozzarella, rocket and smearings of tapenade or a drizzle of olive oil. Grill or griddle till cheese is soft and melty.

Tuna & Mash Dressed up in Tomato

For 2
2 tuna steaks, each
    175 g/6 oz in weight
Olive oil
Garlic, peeled
Mash
450 g/1 lb potatoes
1 clove garlic, peeled
55 ml/2 fl oz milk
25 g/1 oz butter
Lemon juice
Any herb
Salt and black pepper
Drizzle
1 tsp Dijon mustard
Pinch sugar
1 tbsp red wine or sherry
    vinegar
55 ml/2 fl oz olive oil
Pinch of salt
2–3 tomatoes, chopped
6 black olives, chopped
    (optional)
1–2 tbsps dill chopped,
    (optional)

variations
TOMATO DRESSED
SALMON
At STEP 7 brush
salmon fillets with a
mix of soy, sugar and
Chinese rice wine or
rice vinegar. At STEP
9 top with tomato
drizzle and bits of
sushi ginger.
ANOTHER LAYER
Top tuna or salmon
with a mix of crème
fraîche and chopped
spring onion.

Simply lovely. Simply healthy. Fresh tomato in a punchy dressing lifts griddled tuna beautifully…

Method
1. **Mash:** Bring a pan of lightly salted water to boil. Peel potatoes and cut into large chunks. Add to water with garlic.
2. Boil for 20 minutes or till tender. Test by poking the spuds with a knife.
3. Drain. Slap back into the warm pan on a low heat. Shake the pan to dry them for a minute without scorching.
4. Add the milk and butter to the pan to warm. Remove. Mash the spuds and garlic with a masher or fork till ultra smooth. Add a good squeeze of lemon juice, any herb and lots of seasoning. Cover and keep warm.
5. **Drizzle:** Whisk the mustard, sugar, vinegar, oil and salt together. Add the tomatoes and olives and dill if using.
6. **Tuna:** Rub a griddle pan very lightly with oil. Put it on to heat.
7. Mix the olive oil and garlic. Rub it into and over the tuna.
8. Slap the fish onto a sizzling hot griddle. Press down with a fish slice so it marks up well. Cook for 2–3 minutes per side but never overdo. Tuna is at its most tender when still pink in the middle.
9. **Assemble:** Slap a heap of lovely creamy mash on each plate. Stick the fish on there. Drizzle tomato dressing over the top. Perfect with green leaves and green beans.

Sexy Tomato & Mushroom on Polenta

I reckon this makes a perfect summer dish. Tomatoes are definitely at their best when they're just picked. Crisp griddled polenta is well easy and makes an impressive addition. This is simple to make yet chic and delicious.

Method

1. Polenta: Boil the water and salt in a large pan. Add polenta in a steady stream. Stir with a long-handled spoon or whisk. Caution. It spits and bubbles. Reduce heat. Simmer for 5 minutes. Add butter and cheese and herbs if using.

2. Pour while hot into a lightly-oiled tin approximately 28 x 18 x 4 cm/11 x 7 x 1¼ in, or over greaseproof paper. Leave to cool.

3. Chill in fridge if not using immediately. Cut into fingers or squares when ready.

4. Topping: Sit the tomato and mushrooms in a baking dish. Mix the garlic into the olive oil. Brush over the vegetables. Leave to marinate for a while or use immediately.

5. Preheat oven to 200°C/400°F/gas 6.

6. Bake the tomato and mushrooms for 15 minutes.

7. Meantime, heat a griddle pan till well hot. Brush polenta squares with olive oil. Slap them onto the griddle to sizzle. Don't turn till crisped and marked up. Cook on all sides.

8. Assemble: Put a slice of polenta on each plate. Top with rocket, mushroom and tomato. Drizzle with a little balsamic and oil.

For 2
Polenta
½ tsp salt
1.2 litres/2 pints water
200 g/7 oz fastcook polenta
50 g/2 oz butter
2 handfuls grated Parmesan (optional)
2 tbsps chopped sage or rosemary (optional)

Topping
1 large tomato, sliced in half
2 field mushrooms
1 clove crushed garlic
Olive oil
Handful rocket
Balsamic vinegar

Cheese

Henry's the biggest cheese fan I've ever met. A visit to his place means compulsory cheese tasting sessions. But weirdly enough he never cooks with it. Why? In my book it's a cracking ingredient. Cheese does stuff nothing else can – melting down in a beautiful gooey style making the best of itself and working as the main feature or sitting in the background holding it together. So grate it, slice it, melt it or spread it. Crumble it. Chew it. Make it. Bake it. All that calcium and protein's really good for you. Stick it on bread & crackers. Slap it on pizzas, chuck it on salads. Feature it in my Lancashire cheeseburgers. In a classic tart or two. Sharpen up a Greek filo pie with it. Whack it into French-style Yorkshire, lovely

Swiss cheese fondue. Check out the cool Cheddar, chilli & onion muffins. Sort your own dairy – make your own cream cheese. Try a range of cheeses. Preferably local. Check out the weird names for a good bit of comedy. Visit the deli and the farmers' market. You'll meet some great people who know about food and get some free tasting sessions. Enjoy yourself.

For 1 ball
600 ml/1 pint natural yogurt
1 tsp salt

Eat with:
Olive oil for drizzling
Scoops – celery, carrot,
chicory leaves.

Spreads – on bread and
crackers; in cream cheese
and cucumber sandwiches;
thick layers on bread; with
own raspberry jam (pg 138).

Drizzle – with honey on a
sliced fruit plate.

---

variation
SWEET CHEESE
CRÊPES
Slap caster sugar to
taste in some cheese.
Spoon into a hot plain
or choc crêpe (pg 111).
Drizzle with maple
syrup and raspberries.

Cracking Cream Cheese

Sounds tricky? Don't you believe it. Making your own cream cheese is so easy. Customize with herbs or garlic or eat as is. Team with homestyle bread or my poppyseed crackers. PS Make overnight for a quality breakfast.

Method

1. Sit large sieve or colander over a bowl. Line with a square of muslin (at least $1/2 \times 1/2$ m/18 x 18 in diameter).

2. Stir salt into yogurt (in tub or measuring jug). Tip into muslin.

3. Either: Leave in a cool place while the liquid (whey) drips through into the bowl leaving the cheese (curds) in the sieve. **Or:** Bring ends of muslin together. Tie over a tap so liquid drips into the sink.

4. Leave for 6 hours or overnight. Enjoy as is or customize it. Sorted.

Homestyle Poppyseed Crackers

Well impressive. Cracking crackers (excuse the cheesy pun). Snack on these cheeky little biscuits any time you like. Perfect with toppings or dips for partying. Cheese & crackers is a classic pleaser...

Method

1. Preheat oven to 150°C/300°F/gas 2. Grease 2 large baking trays.

2. Sift flour, baking powder and salt into a big bowl. Chuck butter in.

3. Use your fingertips to rub butter lightly into the flour till invisible. Stir in poppy seeds.

4. Add cream and water (you may not need it all) with a fork for a firm dough. Less water makes a crisper cracker.

5. Roll out thinly on a lightly floured board with a floured rolling pin. Prick all over with a fork to stop it puffing when cooking.

6. Cut into cracker shapes. Cook on baking trays for 25–30 minutes or till crisp and only just coloured. Cool on rack. Store in something airtight. Easy.

Makes 20

225 g/8 oz plain white flour
1/2 tsp baking powder
1/2 tsp salt
25 g/1 oz butter and extra for greasing
1 tbsp black poppy seeds
1 1/2 tbsps single cream
5–6 tbsps water

variations

SALTY
Sprinkle with a bit of sea salt before baking.
ROSEMARY
Substitute chopped rosemary for poppy seeds.
CELERY
Season with 1/2 tsp celery salt in place of ordinary.

White Cottage Loaf

For 1 large loaf
675 g/1 1/2 lb strong white
   bread flour
1 tsp salt
1 tsp sugar
10 g/1/2 oz butter
1 x 7 g sachet dried yeast
425 ml/3/4 pint warm water
Beaten egg and milk for
   brushing (optional)
Extra flour for dusting
   (optional)

variations
NEAT PEOPLE'S
LOAF
At STEP 7 slap the
dough into a greased
900 g/2 lb loaf tin.

PLAIT
At STEP 7 divide the
dough into three
sausages. Join at one
end and plait together.

Well old-style. This classic loaf shows off top cheeses (and cheers up average stuff). Think fantastic texture and awesome taste combo. Shape how you want it. Slap on the butter & chutney.

Method
1. Sift flour, salt and sugar into a big bowl. Chuck butter in.
2. Rub into flour between fingertips till invisible.
3. Tip yeast in. Add water gradually, mixing with your hands or a metal spoon. Pull into a soft dough adding a bit more water or flour if needed.
4. **Either:** Knead in an electric mixer with dough hook for 5 minutes.
Or: Punch, slap, stretch and knead by hand on a floured board for an 8 minute workout till pliable.
5. Rest dough to rise in a large bowl somewhere warm. Cover with a tea towel or carrier bag. Leave till doubled in size.
6. Sit dough back on the board. Knead again for a minute.
7. Cut and shape two-thirds of the dough into a large bun shape. Sit on a lightly floured baking tray with the final third shaped into a smaller bun on top. Stick a wooden spoon handle down through the centre to bond the two.
8. Cover with a loose carrier or other. Leave to rise for 20 minutes.

Preheat oven to 230°C/450°F/gas 8.
9. **Crunchy crust:** Brush with beaten egg and milk mix.
Soft crust: Sprinkle a bit of flour over it. **Seed crust:** Sprinkle with poppy or sesame seeds.
10. Bake for 30–40 minutes. Stick greaseproof on top if it browns up too fast. Tap bottom (should sound hollow). Give longer if needed. Cool on rack. Eat with butter … and cheese … and whatever…

Irish Soda Bread

A cool swap for regular bread if you're short on time and fancy a fizz (the buttermilk does it). Made from scratch – no rising – in 40 minutes. Perfect match with hard and soft cheeses. Awesome warm with own jam and butter.

Method
1. Preheat oven to 220°C/425°F/gas 7.
2. Sift flours, cream of tartar, bicarb and salt into a large bowl.
3. Slap butter in. Rub it into the flour lightly between your fingers till it's invisible.
4. Dent the mix. Stir buttermilk into the dent a bit at a time, incorporating the flour as you go for a soft dough. Add a splash more liquid if needed. Pull dough together gently.
5. Sit it on a lightly floured board. Handling gently (no kneading) shape it into a round loaf. Mark into 4 sections by cutting a cross into the top with a knife or press across with the handle of a wooden spoon.
6. Bake on a lightly greased baking tray for 25–30 minutes or till the loaf looks done and sounds hollow when you tap the base.
7. Cool on a rack. Break into sections for serving. Best eaten same day.

Makes 1 loaf
250 g/9 oz plain white flour
250 g/9 oz wholemeal flour
2 tsps cream of tartar
2 tsps bicarbonate of soda
1 tsp salt
50 g/2 oz soft butter
300 ml/10 fl oz buttermilk
  (you may need a bit
  more)

variations
SODA WHITE
Use all white flour.
SODA BROWN
Use all wholemeal.

Spanakopita: Greek Cheese Filo Pie

Eat it with mates. Make it with mates. Laying out the filo is a two-person job. This crisp filo pie has the distinctive taste of salty Feta with loads of spinach and garlic.

Method

1. Preheat oven to 230°C/450°F/gas 8.
2. **Filling:** Heat oil in a big saucepan or casserole. Cook onion and garlic gently. Stir with a wooden spoon for 5 minutes or till soft, not coloured.
3. Pile spinach in. It looks mountainous but wilts fast. Stir to coat. Soften for 2 minutes.
4. Tip into a big bowl with Feta, nutmeg, salt and pepper.
5. **Pie base:** Melt the butter in a pan gently without colouring. Get a pastry brush.
6. Open filo. Sit it on a board or plate. Cover with a tea towel or cloth to keep it usable.
7. Butter base and sides of a 23 cm/9 in loose-bottomed tart tin. Lay the first sheet across it. Brush immediately with butter. Lay the next sheet across it to make the shape of a cross. Brush with butter. Repeat the pattern until 5 sheets used.
8. **Fill it:** Discard any liquid from the spinach/cheese mix. Spoon filling over pie base.
9. **Top it:** Lay a new sheet of filo across the pie. Brush with butter. Fold edges down and in to seal the top and base together.
10. Lay another sheet to make the shape of a cross again. Butter. Fold down and in. Repeat with another 3 sheets till covered.
11. Remove tart rim carefully. Put pie on its base onto a baking tray.
12. Brush top with butter. Sprinkle with poppy seeds and sea salt.
13. Bake for 15 minutes or till crisp and golden. Eat hot, warm or cold.

For 4

- 1–2 tbsps olive oil
- 1 medium–large onion, finely chopped
- 3 cloves garlic, peeled and crushed
- 450 g/1 lb baby or regular spinach leaves, any tough stalks removed
- 350 g/12 oz Feta cheese, crumbled
- Grated fresh nutmeg
- Salt and black pepper
- 25 g/1 oz butter
- 225 g/8 oz pack of filo pastry (10 sheets at least)
- Poppy seeds and sea salt for topping

Eat with:

Tzatziki (pg 140)
Baba ganoush (pg 90)
Greek salad: Chopped tomatoes, olives and cucumber in olive oil and lemon dressing
Hummus (pg 140)

350 g/12 oz potatoes, peeled
1 tbsp olive oil
Sea salt
1 tbsp butter
2 white fish fillets, skin on
(cod, haddock or coley,
175 g/6 oz or big as
you like)
1–2 tbsps good bought or
homestyle pesto (pg 139)
3–4 tbsps grated Parmesan
Tin of mushy peas
Juice of 1 lemon
A bit of fresh mint, finely
chopped (optional)

variations
TOMATO & PESTO
At STEP 6 spread a
little lush tomato
sauce or passata on
half the fillet.
SWEET POTATO
CHIPS
Peel sweet potatoes.
Cut into chunks. Toss
in sunflower oil and a
bit of sea salt. Bake till
caramelized. Lovely.

Fish & Chips & Yorkshire Caviar

Another fine multicultural feast. If you can't get to the
sea – make this. You'll be there. Tasty Italian pesto and
Parmesan lift the fish. Big chips and peas bring it home.
Not a Parmesan fan? Stretch for the Cheddar…

Method
1. Preheat oven to 220°C/425°F/gas 7.
2. **Chips:** Boil potatoes for 10 minutes. Drain. Cut into large oven
chips. Roll them in the olive oil and sea salt.
3. Lay on a baking tray. Cook for 30–40 minutes.
4. **Fish:** Ten minutes before you eat, melt oil and butter in a frying pan
till hot. Fry the fish, skin side down for 3–4 minutes till it's crispy.
5. Move the fish carefully onto to a baking tray, using a fishslice.
6. Spread a thin layer of pesto over the top of each fillet. Sprinkle
generously with freshly grated Parmesan.
7. Cook in the oven for 5 minutes or till white and cooked through and
flaky. Pierce with a knife to check. (Larger portions can take way longer.)
8. **Mushy peas:** Warm through adding a good spritz of fresh lemon
and a bit of mint. Eat with chips, homestyle tomato ketchup (pg 139)
and a bit of malt vinegar.

Swiss Cheese Fondue

Creamy, cheesy, dead luxurious. Fondue's a posh cheese sauce to dunk chunks of bread in. It's speedy to prep and easy to do. Get a load of mates round for a fondue party.

Method

1. Prepare all ingredients and accompaniments before you get cooking.
2. Rub cut garlic all round the inside of a saucepan or fondue pot.
3. Tip wine in and put on hob. Heat till it just simmers. Don't rush it.
4. Add cheese bit by bit, stirring constantly with a wooden spoon. It takes time to melt down to a smooth sauce between additions.
5. Put Kirsch or water into a small bowl with cornflour. Mix together.
6. When the fondue mix eventually bubbles (don't let it burn) stir in liquid cornflour, pepper and nutmeg. Keep stirring as it thickens.
7. Very carefully carry fondue pot over to the lit burner on the table. Take spoon so you can stir. Sit it over a low heat.
8. Sit. Stick warmed bread onto fondue forks. Dunk. Eat 'em.

For 4
1 large clove garlic, halved
300–400 ml/$^1/_2$–$^3/_4$ pint white wine
275 g/10 oz Gruyère cheese and 275 g/10 oz Emmenthal cheese, grated
1 tbsp Kirsch or water
1 tbsp cornflour
Black pepper
Freshly grated nutmeg
Best baguette or crusty bread in bite-sized cubes

Other dunkers
Boiled new or fingerling potatoes.

Eat with:
Tomato & onion salad (pg 140)
Green salad (pg 140)

Brilliant White Pizza

For 2

Pizza bases
2–4 frozen pizza bases
   or make fresh:
450 g/1 lb strong white
   bread flour
1 tsp salt
1 tsp caster sugar
2 x 7 g sachet fast action
   dried yeast
300 ml/¹/₂ pint warm water
2 tbsps good olive oil

Topping
Olive oil
Cut clove of garlic
2 balls Mozzarella
Sea salt

Side
2 fresh tomatoes, chopped
A few black olives
Glug of olive oil
Drizzle of balsamic vinegar
Handful of rocket or spinach

Eat with:
Green salad (pg 140)
Courgette ribbon salad (pg 141)

---

variation

FOUR CHEESE
At STEP 7, spread garlicky tomato sauce (pg 55) over each base. Cover each quarter with a grated cheese of choice, e.g. Gruyère, Mozzarella, Parmesan, Cheddar. At STEP 8, bake for 10–12 minutes or till crisp and bubbling.

Some people like their pizza with a load of tomato. Others like it with less. Doing it this way will please everyone. It's simple yet sophisticated. Get out the candles – eat pure white pizza.

Method

1. **New dough:** Sift flour and salt into a bowl. Add sugar, yeast, water and oil. Mix to a soft dough with your hand or wooden spoon. Add more water or flour if needed.

2. **Knead using food mixer:** Use dough hook for 8 minutes. **By hand:** Slap dough onto a floured board. Pull, stretch and punch using the heel of your hand for 8–10 minutes to get it soft and elastic.

3. Put dough into a bigger bowl. Cover with a carrier bag/tea towel. Leave in a warm place for 1 hour or till doubled in size.

4. Lightly oil 2–4 large baking/pizza trays. Sit dough on board. Knead for 2 minutes. Cut into 2 or 4. Roll or punch and stretch each out thinly for bases.

5. Lay on trays. Leave covered to rise for 15–20 minutes.

6. Preheat oven to 250°C/475°F/gas 9.

7. **Top:** Brush fresh or own frozen bases with a bit of oil. Rub with cut garlic. Slice Mozzarella thinly. Lay over bases with spaces for spreading.

8. Drizzle with a bit of oil and sprinkle of sea salt. Bake for 15 minutes or till base is crisp, top melted and just colouring.

9. **Side:** Meantime mix extra bits. Sit to side of white pizza.

Cheese & Potato Pizza

A bit like Henry and music – these tastes go together. Think thin crispy pizza base with a meltingly soft top. This comforting pizza's pretty spectacular.

Method

1. Make fresh pizza dough (pg 34) risen till the end of STEP 3.
2. **Topping:** Boil potato slices for 5 minutes. Don't let them break up. When just softening (test with a knife) drain well.
3. Gently fry onion in oil till just soft, not coloured.
4. **Top:** Slap home frozen bases onto baking trays or get fresh bases. Spread onion then crème fraîche and herbs evenly over them.
5. Top with potato slices. Layer sliced cheeses over and in between spuds with optional sliced artichoke. Finish with more herbs, seasoning, Parmesan and a little olive oil.
6. Bake for 10–15 minutes or till base is crisp, top bubbling.

For 2
2 own frozen pizza bases
    or fresh (pg 34)
Pinch of salt
2 large unpeeled potatoes
    (Maris Pipers or King
    Edwards work) in
    5 mm/¼ in slices, or
    6–8 salad spuds
1 medium onion, thinly
    sliced
3–4 tbsps olive oil and
    extra for drizzling
3 tbsps low-fat crème
    fraîche
Fresh thyme or oregano
Artichoke heart from a deli
    counter or jar (optional)
1 ball Mozzarella, thinly
    sliced
75 g/3 oz Gruyère, thinly
    sliced
Freshly grated Parmesan
Salt and pepper

Eat with:
Coleslaw (pg 141)
Watercress or rocket
Tomato salad (pg 140)
Orange salad (pg 140)
Roast pepper salad (pg 140)

variation
DIFFERENT TOPPERS
Try tucking any of these into your topping: sundried tomatoes, smoked ham, pancetta, olives, rosemary.

Sfinciuni – Cheese Pizza Pasty

For 1
1 small piece of pizza dough (pg 34, risen to end of STEP 3)
1–2 tbsps passata with a little crushed garlic, or tomato sauce (pg 55)
Bits of cooked ham, bacon or salami
A few pitted olives
Any cheese, sliced or grated
Fresh basil
Parmesan, freshly grated
Olive oil
Sea salt

Eat with: Coleslaw (pg 141).

Pizza or pasty? Who cares? With brilliant tastes like these there's no need to shell out for inferior bought pizza – or pasty. Perfect for snacks, meals, pack-ups…

Method

1. Roll dough out thinly to a large rectangle on floured board.

2. Smear passata or tomato sauce thinly over the lower half.

3. Scatter own selection of meat, olives, cheese, herbs, Parmesan and a drizzle of olive oil over sauce. Fold top half over lower half. Press edges of pasty down to seal (use a bit of water if needed).

4. Leave to rise in a warm place for 15 minutes.

5. Meantime, preheat oven to 220°C/425°F/gas 7.

6. Brush pasty with a bit of oil. Sprinkle sea salt. Bake on a lightly oiled tray for 10–15 minutes or till cooked through.

variation

CHEESE 'N' HAM PASTY

Use all-butter puff pastry in place of pizza dough. Roll out thinly as you would the pizza. Spread a little mustard on the bottom half. Cover with grated cheese, ham, more grated cheese. Fold and brush with beaten egg and milk. Bake for 15–20 minutes. Good with a salad.

French-Style Yorkshire (Gougère)

Two great cuisines collide. Yorkshire's best meets French chic. Tasty stringy cheese melts down into best batter. Scoff with salad or slice up for parties.

Method

1. Whisk eggs, salt and milk furiously together with a hand whisk or electric mixer (whisk attachment). Leave 30 minutes if possible. Meantime, preheat oven to 220°C/425°F/gas 7.
2. Tip 2 tablespoons of oil into an enamel dish or tin (25 x 18 x 8 cm/ 10 x 7 x 3 in). Slap into oven in advance. You want it sizzling.
3. Whisk sifted flour into milk till smooth then add 2 tablespoons of oil. Whisk thoroughly.
4. Add diced cheese to batter.
5. Pour into searing hot oil in tin. Cook for 35 minutes or till pud is golden-topped and well risen. Chop into squares and scoff (it's rich). Or eat bigger chunks with chutney and salad.

For 4
2 eggs
Pinch of salt
225 ml/8 fl oz milk
4 tbsps sunflower oil
75 g/3 oz plain flour
225 g/8 oz Gruyère cheese,
   diced into small cubes

Eat with:
Good apple chutney for dipping (pg 139)
Tomato & onion salad (pg 140)
Green salad (pg 140) with sharp dressing (make it heavy on the chicory)

Classic Cheese & Onion Tart

For 4–6
Pastry
See pg 138
Filling
1 tbsp light olive oil
50 g/2 oz butter
3 large onions (about
  700 g/1½ lbs), thinly
  sliced
2 cloves garlic, crushed
3 eggs, beaten
200 ml/7 fl oz double or
  sour cream
75 g/3 oz grated Gruyère
  or Cheddar
Salt and pepper

variation
CHEESE, ONION &
ASPARAGUS TART
At STEP 5 lightly fry
1 sliced medium onion
with a large bunch of
sliced spring onions till
just soft. Steam or boil
10 asparagus spears till
just tender. At STEP 6
mix the onion mix into
the cheese and cream.
At STEP 7 lay half the
filling in the tart, then
the cooked asparagus
like wheel spokes, then
remaining filling.

This tart's a classic. A gorgeous mix of melted cheese and soft sweet onions. Team with stuffed baked spuds and awesome salads.

Method
1. Make pastry: By hand or processor.
2. Grease a 23 cm/9 in loose-based tart tin.
3. Roll pastry out lightly on a floured board. Make it big enough to fit the base plus sides of the tin.
4. Line tin: Ease one edge of the pastry off the board. Roll the pin underneath to the centre then use it to lift pastry up and over the tin. Let pastry down onto tin then roll pin away carefully. Mould pastry gently into the tin. Fill any gaps with extra pastry. Press tears together. Chill for 30 minutes.
5. Filling: Melt oil and butter in a large pan or casserole over low heat. Cook onions and garlic very slowly (20–30 minutes) till very soft but uncoloured. Preheat oven to 200°C/400°F/gas 6.
6. Slap onions in a bowl to cool for a bit. Beat eggs, cream, cheese and seasoning together. Mix with onions.
7. Tip mix into the tart. Bake for 30 minutes or till pastry is cooked and filling risen and golden. Let it settle for 10 minutes before eating.

Lancashire Cheeseburgers

Who says burgers need meat? Here's the ultimate tasty cheeseburger. Lancashire's sharpness of flavour cooks up well. Get colour and creativity into your stacking.

Method

1. Blitz the bread to make crumbs. Tip them into a large bowl with the cheese, onion, gram flour and herbs.

2. Add the egg, mustard, lemon rind and seasoning. Mix with a fork. Chill the mix in the fridge till needed.

3. Sort the mayos and stacking ingredients before you start to cook.

4. Heat a little oil in a frying pan. Divide the mix into 6 flat burgers. Fry gently for 4 minutes each side or till cooked through and golden.

5. **Either:** Eat bread-free on a pile of any green leaves with apple chutney, ketchup and mayos for dipping. **Or:** Eat breaded in warm buns, pittas or on griddled focaccia with rocket, tomato, red onion and mashed avocado mayo.

variations

CHILLI CHEESE
At STEP 1 chop in a red chilli.
GREEK BURGER
Use Feta cheese instead of Lancashire and add in a few chopped black olives.

Makes 6
110 g/4 oz white crustless bread
175 g/6 oz Lancashire cheese, grated
1 medium onion, finely chopped
2 tbsps gram flour
1–2 tbsps fresh mint, basil, dill, parsley or coriander
1 large egg
1 tsp English mustard
Lemon rind
Salt and black pepper
Sunflower oil

Dipping
Green salad leaves
Apple chutney (pg 139)
Ketchup (pg 139)
Mayos (pg 139)

Stacking
Buns, pittas, or focaccia
Rocket
Thinly sliced tomato
Sliced red onion

Mashed avocado mayo
Mash half a ripe avocado into 3 tbsps mayo. Mix in a crushed garlic clove and a squeeze of lemon.

Blue Cheese Salad

For 2
Garlic croutons
1 clove garlic, crushed
1 tbsp olive oil
50 g/2 oz crustless bread, diced
Salad
1 Cox's apple
Little lemon juice
Cos or little gem lettuce
2 crisp sticks celery
1 head chicory
Few rocket or spinach leaves
Few walnuts (optional)
Dressing
110 g/4 oz Roquefort cheese, crumbled
50 ml/2 fl oz best mayo or own (pg 139)
100 ml/3½ fl oz low fat crème fraîche
1 tsp Dijon mustard
1 pinch caster sugar
1 clove garlic, crushed
1 tbsp lemon juice

Eat with: Warm crusty homemade bread (pg 28) or good bought bread.

A French hero. Powerful flavours of garlic and Roquefort complement the crunchy textures in this fit creamy salad. PS I wouldn't recommend this one before a date – unless you're both eating it…

Method
1. Preheat oven to 180°C/350°F/gas 4.
2. **Garlic croutons:** Mix the garlic and oil in a bowl. Put the cubes of bread in to coat. Slap them on a flat baking tray. Crisp in the oven for 8–10 minutes.
3. **Salad:** Chop apple into small dice. Toss in a bit of lemon juice (stops browning). Chuck it in a bowl with thinly sliced celery, chopped chicory, salad leaves and optional nuts.
4. **Dressing:** Tip half the Roquefort into a blender, processor or bowl. Blend or mash with other ingredients for smooth or rough texture. Taste. Adjust seasoning, adding a splash more water or juice if you like it thinner.
5. Slap salad onto plates. Pour dressing over half the leaves. Crumble remaining cheese over the lot with croutons. Store excess dressing in jar and fridge it.

variations
At STEP 3 add any of the following:
BLOODY MARY
3 diced sundried tomatoes and ½ tsp celery salt.
BIG ONION & GARLIC
3 gently fried tbsps.
CHORIZO
3 diced and fried slices.
PANCETTA
3 crisp diced and fried slices.
HAM & OLIVE
2 diced slices and pitted olives.
CREAMY
1 tsp cream cheese buried in each muffin.

Cheddar, Chilli & Onion Muffins

Who says muffins have to be sweet? Grate a strong Cheddar into this top savoury mix. Great for late breakfasts and break time snacks. Stick a few in your sports bag (don't crush 'em).

Method

1. Preheat oven to 190°C/375°F/gas 5. Meantime, tip the flour, baking powder, sugar, salt, cayenne and mustard into a bowl.

2. Melt the butter gently in a small pan. Whisk the eggs and milk together in another bowl. Add the warm (not hot) melted butter.

3. Tip this liquid mix into the flour with the cheese, onion, chilli and herbs. Using a large metal spoon, fold the ingredients until they just come together. Don't beat the mix. You want to retain air. The odd lump is cool.

4. Split the mix between 12 large muffin cases sitting in a muffin tin. Sprinkle Parmesan on top. Bake 20–30 minutes or till well risen and golden.

Makes 12

275 g/10 oz plain white flour, sifted
3 tsps baking powder
1 tbsp sugar
½ tsp salt
Good pinch of cayenne pepper
Pinch of dry mustard
50 g/2 oz butter
3 eggs
200 ml/7 fl oz milk
150 g/5 oz very strong Cheddar, grated
4 spring onions, finely sliced
1 small red chilli, de-seeded and finely chopped
Fresh parsley, thyme or coriander
Grated Parmesan for topping

Eat with:
Soup
A bit of salad in a pack-up

Pasta

Ariyo's a right pasta fan. Sometimes he'll have it three times a day when there's a game coming up, when he's training or generally knackered. It gives him the energy he needs to excel at his sport. Plus it's relaxing (the starch does it). Pasta's an easy speedy thing to cook. Ideal for when he's been training and bussed it back home of a night. Don't think you need to be slapping fresh pasta together every time. Dried stuff from the deli or supermarket works a treat. I've included the real deal for when you've the time and fancy a challenge. Vary your pasta (there're so many). Always cook it in shedloads of lightly salted boiling water (it spreads). Sort a range of tasty real sauces so you're never bored. Ariyo's top sauce involved opening a jar a while back – now he's into creamy

mushroom tagliatelle and garlic bread. Sausage ragu on penne (for breakfast). Old family favourites like macaroni cheese. Crunchy garlic breadcrumb linguine. Angel hair frittata. Pasta al forno. Penne puttanesca. Team your pastas with some great little salads, crunchy breads and freshly grated Parmesan.

Pasta with Sausage Ragu

For 4

1 tbsp olive oil
1 onion, finely chopped
3 cloves garlic, peeled
  and crushed
1 small red chilli, de-seeded
  and chopped
½ tsp fennel seeds (or
  ground fennel)
6 quality pork or Italian
  sausages
225 g/8 oz chestnut
  mushrooms, roughly
  chopped
150 ml /5 fl oz wine, water
  or stock
1 x 440 g/14 oz can
  chopped tomatoes
1 tsp tomato purée
Pinch of sugar
Squeeze of lemon juice
2 tbsps finely chopped
  parsley, rosemary or basil
Pinch of salt
350 g/12 oz tagliatelle,
  penne or farfalle
Parmesan for sprinkling

I can never quite finish this one no matter how hungry I am. Maybe it's the carbs or the damned fine sauce. Perfect after doing a load of sport. Use quality sausages.

Method

1. Heat oil in a large pan. Chuck in onion, garlic, chilli and fennel seeds. Cook gently till soft and translucent.
2. Cut down the length of each sausage. Strip and discard skin. Crumble or cut meat into the onion.
3. Increase heat. Stir meat till it browns. Decrease heat. Slap in the mushrooms. Cook a further 5–10 minutes, stirring sometimes.
4. Increase heat. Add wine, water or stock. Boil for 2–3 minutes. Add tomatoes, purée, sugar, lemon juice and herbs.
5. Boil for 1 minute. Reduce heat. Simmer very gently for 15–20 minutes. Stir once or twice. Add a splash of liquid if it dries out.
6. Meantime cook pasta in a large pan of lightly salted boiling water as packet instructions. Drain in colander. Pour boiling water over. Drain. Slap back in the pan with an optional bit of oil or butter.
7. Stir sauce in or serve on top of pasta. Eat with freshly grated Parmesan, bread and sharply dressed green salad.

Mushroom Pasta & Garlic Bread

If you're into your mushrooms this is your dish. Easy enough for everyday. Special enough for special occasions.

Method

1. Garlic bread: Preheat oven to 200°C/400°F/gas 6. Chuck the butter and crushed garlic in a bowl. Cream together. Mix in chopped herbs and/or lemon, if using. Slash the loaf diagonally, leaving the pieces attached at the bottom. Spread the garlic butter into the cuts.

2. Wrap the bread in foil. Bake on a tray for 25 minutes.

3. Pasta: Put a large pan of lightly salted water on to boil. Add the pasta when you have a fierce boil. Cook till al dente or as you like it.

4. Sauce: Meanwhile, heat the oil and butter gently in another pan.

5. Slap in the onion and garlic. Cook very gently for 5 minutes till soft

but not coloured. Add the mushrooms. Cook gently until they soften.

6. Increase the heat as you pour in the wine or cider. Let it bubble for 1–2 mins so it reduces by half and the mix looks sticky.

7. Stir in the cream or crème fraîche, reducing the heat. Let it warm through and thicken. Add the parsley or tarragon.

8. Drain your pasta into a colander. Pour boiling water over. Drain well again. Slap it back in the warm pan.

9. Chuck the mushroom cream over it and mix gently. Plate it. Sprinkle with the Parmesan. Eat with garlic bread.

For 2
Pinch of salt
225 g/8 oz tagliatelle
Garlic bread
1 stick French bread
Lots of soft butter
2–3 garlic cloves, peeled and crushed
Fresh herbs (optional)
Squeeze of lemon (optional)
Sauce
1 tbsp olive oil
25 g/1 oz butter
1 small onion or 2 shallots, finely chopped
2 cloves garlic, crushed
275 g/10 oz white or chestnut mushrooms, sliced
125 ml/4 fl oz white wine or cider
75 ml/3 fl oz double cream or crème fraîche
Fresh parsley or tarragon, finely chopped
Parmesan, freshly grated

why not?

Make cheese garlic mushrooms on toast. Make up half the mix. Stick it on a piece of baked bread. Top with grated Gruyère. Stick it under the grill in a small heatproof dish till bubbling.

Spaghetti with Oil, Garlic & Chilli

For 2

225 g/8 oz spaghetti or
   linguine
Salt and black pepper
4 tbsps extra virgin olive oil
2–3 cloves garlic, peeled
   and finely chopped
   or crushed
1–2 red chillies, de-seeded,
   very finely chopped
Handful flatleaf parsley,
   finely chopped

variation
CHILLI POMODORO
At STEP 3 add 225 g/
8 oz chopped cherry
tomatoes, pinch of
sugar, chopped parsley
(or basil, thyme,
oregano, rosemary).
Cook till tomatoes
heat through.
Great with croutons
(pg 10) or garlic
breadcrumbs (pg 47).

The simplicity of this dish is unbelievable, considering the amount of flavour it gives out. Chilli gives the pasta a useful kick. Pro-chefs make this for a workday lunch. Great to impress with little hassle.

Method
1. Boil up a large covered pan of salted water.
2. Add pasta. Cover. Boil again. Uncover. Cook for 10 minutes or till just soft with a bit of bite (al dente) or softer if you like. Test by trying a bit.
3. Meantime, heat olive oil gently in a small pan. Add garlic, chilli and black pepper. Sizzle on a very low heat till soft. Don't let it colour or burn as it will taste bitter. Watch it.
4. Add parsley and salt. Warm through for 15 seconds. Remove from heat.
5. Drain pasta in colander. Pour boiling water over it. Let it drain well.
6. Slap pasta back into the warm pan. Mix the oil in. Serve it.

Crunchy Garlic Breadcrumb Linguine

I love this yummy summery dish. The combo of lemon and crunchy garlic breadcrumbs really works. It's easy to sort out, so get cooking…

Method

1. Put a large covered pan of salted water on to boil while you organize the other ingredients.
2. Add the pasta. Cover to bring to the boil. Remove the lid. Cook for 7–8 minutes till the pasta is al dente or done to your liking.
3. Meantime, heat a little olive oil in a large pan. Fry the bacon or pancetta till crispy. Sit it in a warm place on kitchen paper.
4. **Garlic breadcrumbs:** Blitz the bread into large crumbs in a processor.
5. Take the pan you used to cook your bacon. Put it onto a low heat. Melt the butter and add the crushed garlic.
6. Tip the breadcrumbs in. Fry very gently turning carefully with a spoon till the crumbs are crisp and golden. Keep them warm on a plate.
7. Drain the pasta into a colander. Pour boiling water over it. Let it drain thoroughly. Slap the pasta back into the warm pan.
8. Add a drizzle of olive oil, bacon, tomatoes, herbs, rocket, lemon juice, pepper, half the Parmesan and breadcrumbs. Mix. Serve topped with the remaining crunchy crumbs and Parmesan.

For 2
175 g/6 oz linguine
Little olive oil
4 rashers chopped bacon or 75 g/3 oz cubed pancetta
75 g/3 oz white bread, crusts removed
50 g/2 oz butter
2 cloves garlic, crushed
8–10 cherry tomatoes, halved
2–3 tbsps parsley, chopped
Handful rocket
Juice of half a lemon
50 g/2 oz Parmesan, grated
Salt and black pepper

why not
Slap garlic butter or garlicky tomato sauce on a frozen homestyle pizza base and bake it.

variation
VEGGIE LINGUINE
At STEP 3 slice and fry 175 g/6 oz mushrooms in olive oil and garlic, instead of bacon.

Penne Puttanesca

For 4
3 tbsps olive oil
3 fat cloves garlic, peeled and crushed
1 red chilli, de-seeded and finely chopped
450 g/1 lb ripe tomatoes, roughly chopped or 1 x 440 g tin chopped tomatoes
Pinch of sugar
175 g/6 oz black olives, pitted
1 tbsp capers, drained
6 anchovy fillets
500 g/17 oz penne or spaghetti
2 tbsps torn basil or finely chopped parsley
110 g/4 oz Mozzarella, diced (optional)
Salt and black pepper

Eat with:
Garlic bread (pg 45)
Chicory & watercress salad
Courgette ribbon salad (pg 141)

This one's like the Mediterranean in a bowl. Tomatoes, capers and olives melt down into a thick hardcore sauce that wraps itself around your penne or spaghetti. If you sometimes find pasta can be bland, this is most definitely the one for you.

Method
1. **Sauce:** Heat oil in a large pan over gentle heat. Slap in garlic and chilli. Cook without colouring for 5 minutes or till softening.
2. Add in tomatoes, sugar, olives, capers, black pepper and anchovies.
3. Simmer over a low heat for 20 minutes. You want it thickened. Stir sometimes to avoid sticking.
4. **Pasta:** Boil a large pan of lightly salted water with the lid on. Uncover. Add pasta. Cover and boil again. Uncover and cook for 10 minutes or cooked as you like it.
5. Drain into a colander. Pour boiling water over it. Drain again.
6. Tip pasta back into pan with a bit of olive oil.
7. Stir herbs optional Mozzarella into sauce. Taste. Adjust seasoning.
8. Stir sauce into pasta and plate it or sit on top in bowls.

Angel Hair Frittata

Slice it up for trekking. Al fresco eating. Slapping into pack-ups or really tasty anytime eating. It's a thick omelette crossed with a pasta dish. Angel hair pasta breaks down in the mix, creating a brilliant base for the salty tastes of olive and Feta.

Method

1. Boil a large pan of lightly salted water. Add pasta. Cook till just soft – 2 minutes. Drain. Sit in a bit of cool water.

2. Heat half the oil gently in a 23 cm/9 in pan. Cook onion, garlic and chilli, stirring till softened, not coloured. Tip mix into a large bowl.

3. Drain pasta thoroughly (pat dry if needed). Add to the onion with Feta, Parmesan, spinach or rocket, sour cream, optional olives, eggs and seasoning. Mix well.

4. Heat remaining oil in the onion pan. Pour frittata mix in. Cook over a gentle heat with a lid on for 10 minutes till just set through.

5. Heat grill to medium. Uncover pan and slap on a grill rack to finish cooking (don't melt handle) for a few minutes till soft and golden.

6. Leave to settle. Eat hot, warm or cold with salad.

For 4
100 g/3½ oz angel hair pasta
2 tbsps olive oil
225 g/8 oz onion, thinly sliced
3 cloves garlic, crushed
1 small red chilli, de-seeded and finely chopped
200 g/7 oz pack Feta cheese
25 g/1 oz Parmesan, grated
60 g/2½ oz spinach or rocket
150 ml/5 fl oz sour cream
A few black olives (optional)
6 eggs, beaten
Salt and black pepper
Ground nutmeg (optional)

Eat with:
Green salad (pg 140)
Tomato salad (pg 140)
Tomato & onion salad (pg 140)
Good crusty bread

variation
At STEP 3 add bits of cooked ham or crisply cooked bacon or pancetta.

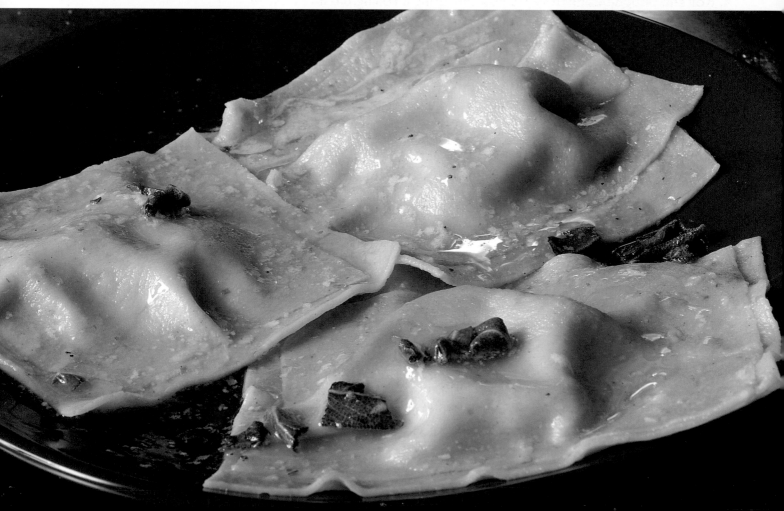

DIY Pasta for Ravioli

I'll put aside an hour or two any time to slap on the music and make my own pasta. Use it to create these gorgeous sweet-tasting ravioli in herb and butter sauce. Feeding the girlfriend? This is well impressive…

Method

1. Pasta: You can mix and pulse the pasta ingredients in a processor but it's best by hand. Sift flour and salt into a large bowl. Make a deep well in the centre. Crack the eggs straight in. Use your hand to beat the eggs then draw in the flour. Keep beating until half the flour is incorporated.

2. Add the olive oil. Keep mixing with your hands until you have a soft stretchy dough and all the flour's all in there.

3. Sit it on a floured board. Knead it as you would for bread. Slap, stretch, pull and roll it with the heel of your hand. After 5–10 minutes you should get a smooth elastic dough. Cover and leave for 20 minutes.

4. Roll the dough out as thinly as you can, using a rolling pin and a bit of stretching. Divide it into long rectangles which are nearly as wide as the roller in your hand pasta machine. Keep rolling if you don't have one.

5. Set the machine up, clamping it to a table leaving both hands free to work. Or get a mate to hold it steady and help roll it.

6. With the roller on its widest setting, insert the end of your first rectangle and roll it on through. Catch the rolled end as it emerges.

7. Reduce the setting on the roller. Roll the piece through another couple of times until it is thin and still strong. Flour lightly if it sticks. If it tears you've over-rolled it. Repeat with the remainder.

8. Divide the thin pasta up into squares approx 7.5 cm/3 in with a sharp knife or pastry cutter. Leave to dry out for 10 minutes.

9. Put a large pan of salted water on to boil for cooking the ravioli.

10. Filling: Mix Ricotta with garlic, seasoning, Parmesan and egg yolk.

11. Sit a teaspoon of the cheese filling in the centre of a pasta square. Put another square on top. Press gently round the mound of filling with your fingertips to seal. Repeat till all the pasta has been used up.

12. Put the ravioli in the boiling water. Cook for 5 minutes or till they rise to the surface. Remove with a slotted spoon. Drain in a colander.

13. Sauce: Working quickly, melt butter gently in a pan. Add lemon juice, sage and seasoning. Pour over the plated ravioli. Scatter with Parmesan.

For 4
Pasta
300 g/10 oz strong plain flour
½ tsp salt
3 large eggs
1 tbsp olive oil
Filling
225 g/8 oz Ricotta
1–2 cloves garlic, crushed
Salt and black pepper
50 g/2 oz Parmesan, grated
1 egg yolk
Sauce
Butter
Juice of 1 lemon
Sage
Salt and pepper
Parmesan

variations
TOMATO PASTA
At STEP 1 add 1 tbsp tomato purée.
TOMATO SAUCE
At STEP 13, add classic tomato sauce (pg 55) instead of herb butter sauce.

why not?
Cut the pasta into a few large sheets to use for lasagne (layer with ragu and top with cheese sauce), or put the pasta through the cutter on your machine for your own tagliatelle.

Gingered-up Sauce with Any Pasta

For 4
2 tbsps olive oil
1 small onion, finely chopped
1–2 cloves garlic, crushed
Small piece of ginger,
  peeled and grated
1 x 400 g/14 oz can chopped
  tomatoes
Pinch sugar
Salt and pepper
Fresh parsley, coriander
  or basil (optional)
Squeeze of lemon juice
Pasta of choice
Little butter (optional)
Freshly grated Parmesan

A bit of ginger lifts a classic tomato sauce. Need I say more? I don't think so. OK – slap it on your best pasta. Grate Parmesan at the table for a top taste and cool ritual…

Method
1. Heat the olive oil in a pan. Add the onion, garlic and ginger. Cook gently for 5 minutes or till soft and translucent.
2. Tip the tomatoes in with the sugar, salt and pepper. Stir and bring to the boil. Reduce the heat immediately. Simmer for 10–15 minutes.
3. Add the herbs, if using, and lemon juice. Taste and adjust seasoning.
4. Meanwhile, put a large covered pan of lightly salted water on to boil. Add your pasta of choice when the water is boiling. Cover as the water returns to a fierce boil. Remove the lid and cook till the pasta is as tender as you like. Refer to instructions on packet.
5. Drain the pasta well and slap it back in the pan with a bit of olive oil or butter. Mix in the sauce. Plate it or serve in bowls.

variations

GINGERED-UP BRUSCHETTAS
Preheat oven to 200°C/400°F/gas 6. Drizzle olive oil over slices of focaccia or good white bread. Bake on a tray till just crisp (5–10 minutes). Layer some gingered-up sauce on top. Top with a bit of your favourite cheese. Bake again till bubbling.

ROAST TOMATO & GINGER SAUCE
Preheat oven to 200°C/400°F/gas 6. Lay whole tomatoes in a roasting tin with sliced garlic and a little grated ginger. Season and drizzle with olive oil. Roast 20–30 minutes or till they blacken. Pull skins off with a fork. Blitz. Pour over pasta with a bit of extra olive oil, fresh torn basil and grated Parmesan.

Good Old Macaroni Cheese

You can't beat it. A favourite in our house and with everyone I know, so it doesn't need much introduction. Just make sure your sauce is properly cheesy and fully-seasoned. Have a go at the green bean spaghetti…

Method

1. Put a large pan of salted water on to boil.
2. Slip the macaroni in. Boil continuously in the uncovered pan till just tender. Drain in a colander and pour boiling water over to stop clumping.
3. Preheat grill or oven to 200°C/400°F/gas 6.
4. **Cheese sauce:** Melt the butter in a small pan over a gentle heat. Add the flour. Stir furiously with a wooden spoon for 2 minutes. Remove from heat. Pour the milk in gradually, beating well with a balloon whisk or spoon as you go to make a smooth thin sauce.
5. Return to the heat. Bring it slowly to the boil while still beating. The sauce will thicken. Add a bit more milk if you think it needs it. Simmer for 2 minutes. Slap in the cheese, mustard, lemon and seasoning. Stir and heat for a further minute. Taste the sauce and adjust the seasoning.
6. Add the macaroni. Pour the mix into an ovenproof dish. Top with extra cheese. Bake for 20 minutes or cook under the grill till golden.

variations

BACON
At STEP 6 add a layer of cooked bacon on top of half the mixture. Top with the rest.
SPINACH
At STEP 6 put a layer of cooked spinach on the base of the dish.
MUSHROOM
At STEP 5 stir in cooked mushroom.
CAULIFLOWER
Cook cauli florets in lightly salted water till tender (8–10 minutes) and substitute for pasta.
BREADCRUMBS
At STEP 6 sprinkle a mix of extra cheese and 1–2 tbsps fresh white breadcrumbs over the top. Bake till bubbling.

For 4
175 g/6 oz macaroni
Cheese sauce
20 g/³/₄ oz butter
20 g/³/₄ oz plain flour
425 ml/³/₄ pint milk
175 g/6 oz grated strong Cheddar or crumbled Lancashire cheese, plus a bit for topping
½ tsp mustard
1 tbsp lemon juice
Salt and black pepper

why not?

Make Green Bean Spaghetti. Push runner beans through a bean shredder. Boil for 3–4 minutes. Drain. Delicious – cutting them this way kind of magnifies the flavour!

Pasta al Forno

Sounds posh but it's not. Al forno means baked. This is just like a lasagne, but using stuffed pasta shells instead of sheets. The cheesy tomatoey sauce is a winner. A great excuse for getting a load of mates round the table.

Method

1. **Beef ragu filling:** Heat the butter and oil gently. Add the onion, celery, garlic and a pinch of salt. Cook very gently over a low heat in a covered pan to sweat the veg for 5–10 minutes.

2. Stir in the bacon. Cook for a minute then increase the heat.

3. Chuck in the mince, stirring till it browns all over.

4. Pour in the wine and let it bubble. Add the stock or water, tomato purée, lemon and seasoning. Boil the mix for a minute then reduce the heat to low. Let it simmer gently for at least 40 minutes, stirring occasionally. Don't let it dry out. Add a bit more liquid if it needs it. Add more purée if it's too sloppy. You want a thick sauce.

5. **Tomato sauce:** Meanwhile, heat oil in another pan. Add the onion or shallot, garlic and a pinch of salt. Cook till soft, not brown.

6. Tip in the tomatoes, sugar, tomato purée, herbs, pepper, pinch of salt and lemon. Boil. Reduce heat. Leave to simmer until serving point, stirring occasionally. Add a little water if it gets too thick.

7. **Pasta:** Cook the pasta shells in plenty of boiling lightly salted water for 10 minutes or till just tender. Drain them well.

8. **To assemble:** Preheat oven to 200°C/400°F/gas 6. Spread a thin layer of tomato sauce over the base of an ovenproof dish.

9. Use a teaspoon to fill each pasta shell or tube with the meat mix. Sit the filled pasta on top of the sauce. Sprinkle a little Parmesan over the top followed by a layer of tomato sauce to cover.

10. Top the lot with a layer of thinly sliced Mozzarella and Parmesan to cover. Cover very loosely with foil. Bake for 30–40 minutes.

For 4–6

Beef ragu filling
25 g/1 oz butter
1 tbsp oil
1 onion, finely chopped
1 stick celery, finely chopped
2 cloves garlic, crushed
2 rashers of bacon, chopped
350 g/12 oz minced steak
50 ml/2 fl oz wine
100 ml/4 fl oz stock or water
2 tsps tomato purée
Squeeze of lemon juice
Salt and black pepper

Classic tomato sauce
1–2 tbsps olive oil
1 small onion or 2 small
   shallots, chopped small
2 cloves garlic, crushed
400 g/14 oz can chopped
   tomatoes
Good pinch of sugar
1 tbsp tomato purée
Fresh basil, or parsley
Salt and black pepper
Squeeze of lemon juice

Pasta
16 conchiglioni (large pasta
   shells) or cannelloni tubes

Topping
3–4 tbsps freshly grated
   Parmesan
2 x 150 g/5 oz balls
   of Mozzarella

variations

Fill shells with
TUNA & RICOTTA
Mix a drained tin of tuna with a tub of Ricotta cheese,
1 crushed garlic clove, a squeeze of lemon and black pepper.
MOZZARELLA & RICOTTA
Mix 1 ball of finely chopped Mozzarella with 1 tub of Ricotta, seasoning and a bit of cooked, diced spinach.

Veg

Warning: this section's not just for vegetarians. Joe loves his meat as much as I do, but when it comes to top tastes he's gone for the green stuff. There's so much out there it's a proper veg field day. Vegetable cooking's a real test of a chef. You need to get creative with combinations of flavours and textures, using herbs and spices with skill and subtlety. This selection's just the tip of the iceberg (lettuce). It's got curries, burgers, chilli tortillas, risotto, moussaka, cool soups, baked chicory, red cabbage, fritters, Sicilian caponata and stand alone veg that are truly magnificent. Joe grows his own 'cos the fresher the better. We're talking health gods remember (that's the veg, not Joe – though he plays a mean game of football). Think fibre, energy, minerals, vitamins to keep you going. No garden? No sweat. Get to farmers' markets, farm shops (Joe works on one in the holidays) or old-style greengrocers. Always sniff and prod veg to check its credentials. Google it to check out when it's in season. No fuss if it's mucky. Buying in supermarkets? Check it's sourced locally, not flown here on holiday.

Leek & Onion Soup

For 4
Soup
1 tbsp butter
Glug of olive oil
350 g/12 oz leeks, thinly
  sliced
2 large French onions,
  peeled and thinly sliced
2–3 cloves garlic, crushed
2 tsps sugar
Salt and pepper
350 ml/12 fl oz dry cider,
  white wine or apple juice
850 ml/1½ pints veg or
  chicken stock (pg 138)
Topping
Baguette or ciabatta, sliced
Harissa mayo
2–3 handfuls grated
  Gruyère or Cheddar

A variation on classic French onion soup. Leeks make it … sweeter. Team with crunchy cheese and harissa croutons. A real winter winner.

Method

1. Melt butter and oil in a large heavy bottomed pan or casserole.
2. Add leeks, onion, garlic and sugar. Stir to coat in oil.
3. Sweat over a low heat with the lid on till well softened, not coloured (10–15 minutes). Add seasoning.
4. Increase heat. Stir the veg till they start to brown up well (don't let them burn).
5. Add cider, wine or juice. Let it bubble. Keep stirring.
6. Add stock (plus extra if needed). Bring soup to the boil for a minute then simmer, covered, on a low heat for at least 20 minutes but give it loads longer for a much deeper flavour. Taste and adjust seasoning.

7. Croutons: Toast slices of good bread or slice and smear with a bit of olive oil. Bake in a hot oven till crisp (5–10 minutes).
8. Mayo: Stir a bit of red harissa into good mayo with crushed garlic and lemon juice.
9. Ladle soup into bowls. Spread croutons with mayo. Top with cheese. Nice one.

Butternut Squash & Ginger Soup

This cheery-up soup offers instant comfort. Butternut squash is so good for you. Thai-style ginger, coconut and lime combo gives it a great kick.

For 4
700 g/1 ½ lbs butternut squash, peeled and cut into large bits
Olive oil
25 g/1 oz butter
1 medium onion, finely chopped
2 fat cloves garlic, crushed
10–12 cm/4–5 in piece of fresh ginger, peeled and grated
Juice of 2 plump limes
850 ml/1½ pints veg stock (pg 138)
50 g/2 oz piece creamed coconut dissolved in 300 ml/½ pint boiling water
2 tsps chopped coriander, plus extra for topping
Salt and pepper
Tabasco sauce (optional)
Balsamic vinegar (optional)

Eat with:
Grated Parmesan
Crumbled cooked pancetta or streaky bacon
Warm soda bread or classic bread and butter

Method

1. Preheat oven to 200°C/400°F/gas 6. Slap the squash on a baking tray. Drizzle with oil. Roast for 30 mins or till soft.
2. Meantime, melt butter gently in a large pan. Fry onion and garlic for 5 minutes or till soft not coloured. Add ginger. Remove from heat.
3. Add cooked squash, lime juice, stock, coconut, coriander, salt and pepper to the mix.
4. Bring to the boil as you stir. Reduce heat. Cover. Simmer gently for 15 mins. Top up with a bit more liquid if it looks too thick.
5. Blitz in a blender or processor. A hand blender works. Taste. Add more seasoning and/or lime, optional shakes of Tabasco and/or balsamic and coriander.

variations
CHILLI IT
Crumble 1–2 dried chillies over the squash before roasting (STEP 1).
SPICE IT
Sprinkle 2 tsps cumin.

Chicory au Gratin

For 4
Juice of 1 lemon
4 chicory heads
1 clove garlic
Soft butter
4 thin slices ham (optional)
1 tbsp Dijon mustard
125 ml/4 fl oz double
   cream or crème fraîche
Salt and black pepper
Gruyère or Parmesan,
   grated
Fresh breadcrumbs
   (optional)

Eat with:
Warm bread to mop juices
Tomato & onion salad (pg 140)
Green salad (pg 140)

variation
BRAISED CHICORY
At STEP 4 melt 1 tbsp
butter in the dish.
Remove. Lay chicory
in it. Season with salt
and pepper, juice of
1/2 lemon, 1/2 tbsp
caster sugar. Lay a bit
of buttered paper
(butter side down) on
top. Cover dish. Bake
at same temp for
30 minutes or till
tender. Eat as above
or as a side dish.

why not?
Chuck uncooked
chicory halves in to
roast for the last 30
minutes with a whole
chicken. The bottom
caramelizes, flavouring
spuds and gravy.

Chicory's slightly bitter so it really does the business in this cheesy, creamy sauce. Makes a great veggie dish (without the ham). Complements a lovely roast chicken.

Method
1. Boil up a pan of water large enough to take all the veg. Add a bit of salt and squeeze of lemon.
2. Boil chicory for 5 minutes. Drain well into a colander. Cool till you can handle. Squeeze excess water out with a tea towel.
3. Preheat oven to 190°C/375°F/gas 5.
4. Rub cut garlic over surface of a shallow baking dish. Butter well all over. Squeeze lemon juice in there.
5. Season chicory with pepper and lemon. Wrap in ham if using.
6. Lay in dish. Cover with a mix of mustard, cream or crème fraîche, and seasoning. Sprinkle with cheese and optional breadcrumbs.
7. Bake for 20–30 minutes till tender (test with a knife), bubbling and golden. Fat chicory may take longer.

Sweetcorn Fritters

These US-style fritters have a bit of bite. Make them work as a snack with dips when you've got mates about or pile 'em high to go with fried chicken or vegetable chilli.

Method

1. Sift flour, salt and paprika into a bowl.
2. Make a dip in the centre. Crack the egg in with a little of the milk. Beat together with a wooden spoon or balloon whisk.
3. Gradually add the rest of the milk, incorporating as you go for a thick smooth batter. Rest it for 30 minutes – unless desperate!
4. Tip the sweetcorn, chilli, pepper and coriander into the batter. Mix gently.
5. Heat the oil in a pan. Drop tablespoons of the fritter mix into the pan. Fry 1–2 minutes each side till the top bubbles and the base is golden. Keep cooked fritters warm while the others are frying.

For 4
50 g/2 oz plain flour
Pinch of salt
Pinch of paprika
1 egg
75 ml/3 fl oz milk
150 g/5 oz can sweetcorn, drained
1 small red chilli, de-seeded and finely chopped
1 red pepper, de-seeded and finely chopped
Fresh coriander
2 tbsps sunflower or olive oil

Eat with:
Guacamole (pg 140)
Sour cream
Salsa (pg 139)
Veggie chilli (pg 65)

Spicy Mushroom 'n' Chickpea Burgers

Makes 6

3 tbsps olive oil
110 g/4 oz onion, finely chopped
2 cloves garlic, peeled and crushed
1 small dried chilli, crumbled
1 tsp ground cumin
1 tsp ground coriander
1/4 tsp turmeric
1 tsp lemon grass paste or 1/2 piece fresh, finely chopped
200 g/7 oz chestnut mushrooms, finely chopped
Juice of 1 lime
Salt and pepper
1 x 400 g/14 oz can chickpeas
75 g/3 oz fresh breadcrumbs
Few shakes Tabasco sauce
2 tbsps fresh coriander, finely chopped
White flour for coating
Olive oil for frying

Stack

Griddled, toasted or warmed bun or ciabatta
Guacamole (pg 140)
Thinly sliced tomato
Mayo mixed with sweet chilli sauce
Rocket
Shredded spring onion

Share a plate of these superior burgers with a group of hardcore meat-eating mates. See if they moan (they won't). They taste a bit like falafel but much better and really work with guacamole.

Method

1. Slap olive oil in a large pan. Heat gently. Add onion and garlic. Cook, stirring for 5 minutes, till softening – not coloured.

2. Chuck in chilli, cumin, coriander, turmeric and lemon grass. Cook for 3 minutes. Add mushrooms and lime. Cook for 5 minutes to soften. Season. Tip into a large bowl to cool a bit.

3. Semi-blitz chickpeas in a processor or crush with a fork till broken, not pasted. Add to bowl with breadcrumbs, Tabasco, coriander, salt and pepper. Mix well with a fork.

4. Scatter coating flour on a large plate. Flour hands. Take handfuls of mix. Shape into 6 burgers. Mould the mix gently. Wash and re-flour hands if they get sticky.

5. Chill burgers on a plate in the fridge for a few minutes or till needed.

6. Fry for 3–4 minutes each side in a little olive oil. Check they're cooked through. Sit on salad leaves or stack 'em.

For 4

2 tbsps sunflower oil
1 large onion, finely chopped
2 fat cloves garlic, peeled and crushed
5 cm/2 in piece fresh ginger, peeled and grated
1 chilli, de-seeded and finely chopped
6 cardamom pods, cracked
3 kaffir lime or curry leaves, crumbled
450 g/1 lb button mushrooms, halved
1 tbsp ground coriander
1 tsp chilli powder
2 tsps cumin
2 good pinches turmeric
1 tsp sugar
200 ml/7 fl oz passata
3 tbsps cream, yogurt or crème fraîche
2 tbsps fresh coriander
Salt and pepper

Eat with
Rice (pg 84)
Naan bread
Poppadoms
Mango chutney
Raita

Mushroom Curry

Mushrooms can be a bit tame but not done this way. There's a lot of spicing in here so taste as you go to check you've got a good balance of flavours.
An awesome curry … add it to your repertoire.

Method

1. Heat the oil in a large pan. Gently sweat the chopped onion for 5 minutes or till softened, but not coloured.
2. Slap in the garlic, ginger, chilli, cardamom and leaves. Stir around for a few minutes. Add the mushrooms and cook gently for 5 minutes.
3. Add the coriander, chilli powder, cumin, turmeric, sugar and passata (or use equivalent amount of chopped tinned tomatoes or fresh).
4. Cover. Simmer gently for 10 minutes.
5. Stir in the cream, yogurt or crème fraîche and coriander. Taste and season with salt and pepper.

why not?

Make some raita. Finely chop a 10 cm/4 in piece of cucumber. Mix with 1 chopped spring onion, 2 crushed garlic cloves, 6 tbsps natural yogurt and seasoning.

variation

CURRY WITH PEAS
Slap in some cooked peas at STEP 5.

For 4

1 big onion, finely chopped
3 cloves garlic, peeled and
  crushed
2½ cm/1 in fresh ginger,
  peeled, roughly grated
1–2 red chillies, de-seeded
  and finely chopped
3 tbsps groundnut or
  sunflower oil
1 tsp ground cumin
1 tsp turmeric
2 tsps ground coriander
1 tsp garam masala
2 ripe tomatoes, chopped
8 tbsps passata
225 ml/8 fl oz water
1 large sweet potato,
  peeled, cubed
1 cauliflower, in florets
1 x 400 g/14 oz can
  chickpeas
Salt
Juice of 1 lemon
Fresh coriander

Eat with:
Basmati rice (pg 84)
Griddled naan bread
Mango chutney
Raita (pg 63)

why not?
Make spinach curry.
Slap 2 bags baby spinach
in a pan with 2 tbsps
water. Wilt for 2
minutes. Drain well.
Squeeze out the
moisture. Stir-fry 1 tsp
mustard seeds in oil for
2 minutes (lid on pan).
Add crushed garlic,
sliced onion and a pinch
of curry powder. Cook
gently till soft. Add
spinach and a bit of salt.
Heat through.

Cool Cauli Curry

One to get down before you escape from home. It
majors in a range of vegetables and chickpeas – great
for protein. Strong on taste. Make a load at the
weekend for weekday eating.

Method

1. Mix the prepped onion, garlic, ginger and chillies together. Or blitz
the lot with a bit of water in a processor.

2. Heat the oil in a large heavy-bottomed pan or casserole. Add onion
mix and stir over a medium heat with a wooden spoon for 2 minutes.

3. Add the cumin, turmeric, ground coriander, garam masala. Stir and
cook for another few minutes.

4. Reduce the heat. Add the fresh tomato. Cook, stirring till it gets pulpy.

5. Pour in the passata and water. Mix well. Now add the sweet potato,
cauliflower and chickpeas.

6. Cover and cook over a gentle heat for 20 minutes or till the
cauliflower is just tender. Add a bit more water if you think it needs it.

7. Remove the lid. Simmer gently for at least 10 minutes so the sauce
reduces. Don't let it dry out. You may want to simmer it a bit longer.

8. Taste. Season with salt, lemon juice and coriander. Keep tasting…

Chilli Pepper & Bean Tortillas

We always use red or orange peppers as a riper pepper gives a sweeter taste. Enjoy this macho chilli wrap which you can griddle, bake or barbie. Cool for lunch and supper. Great for parties.

Method

1. Filling: Slap the oil into a large pan. Fry onions and garlic very gently till softening but not coloured. Stir in the peppers. Cook for 5–8 minutes till softening.
2. Add the chillies, cumin, cayenne (or chilli powder), paprika, sugar, tomatoes, beans, purée, coriander and water. Bring to the boil, stirring.
3. Reduce heat and cover the pan. Simmer the vegetable chilli for 20 minutes. Check it's not sticking and stir occasionally.
4. When sauce is thick, taste and season. Chill till needed.
5. Wrap: Either lay tortillas flat. Spoon a layer of chilli down the centre of each. Sprinkle cheese. Roll wrap round filling. Roll foil round wrap. Slap on very hot griddle for 4 minutes or till cooked through (check). **Or** bake on a tray at 220°C/425°F/gas 7 for 10 minutes (check). Or slap on your barbie. Eat from wrapper.

Makes 12
Bean chilli filling
2 tbsps olive or sunflower oil
1 onion, finely chopped
2 cloves garlic, crushed
1 red pepper and 1 yellow pepper, de-seeded, cored and chopped
2 small red chillies, de-seeded and finely chopped
1 tsp ground cumin
1/2 tsp cayenne or chilli powder
1 tsp paprika
1 tsp caster sugar
1 x 400 g/14 oz can chopped tomatoes
1 x 400 g/14 oz can red kidney beans, drained and rinsed
2 tbsps tomato purée
2 tbsps coriander
125 ml/4 fl oz water
Salt and pepper

12 small soft wraps/tortillas
Cheddar, grated

Eat with:
Guacamole (pg 140)
Sour cream
Salsa (pg 139)

variation
VEGGIE CHILLI ON RICE
At STEP 2 add a splash more water for a looser mix. At STEP 5 serve chilli on bowls of rice, with salsa, grated Cheddar, sour cream and guacamole, with lime to squeeze. Scoop up with soft warmed tortillas and tortilla chips.

For 4

6 tbsps olive oil
2 aubergines cut in
   2 cm/³/₄ in dice
Salt and black pepper
3 sticks celery, thinly sliced
1 large onion, thinly sliced
1x 400 g/14 oz can
   tomatoes or 450 g/
   1 lb fresh, skinned and
   chopped
50 g/2 oz raisins or sultanas
50 g/2 oz green or black
   olives, pitted
1 tsp capers
1–2 tbsps caster sugar
4 tbsps red wine vinegar
2 tbsps parsley, finely
   chopped
2–3 hard-boiled eggs
   (optional)

Eat with:

Warm crusty bread
Salads (pgs 140–141)
Cheeses
Cold deli meats

why not?

Warm any leftovers.
Stir in crème fraîche.
Whack into any pasta
you fancy.

Cracking Caponata

This is a classic Sicilian dish which brings out the best in aubergine. It's sort of sweet and sour but more subtle than that. Serve it as a main course or salad. Scatter with eggs if you want. Whatever, it's special.

Method

1. Heat half the oil in a large pan or casserole dish. Fry the aubergine till soft. Season with a bit of salt and pepper. Cool on kitchen paper.

2. Reduce the heat and slap the celery into the pan. Cook it gently till just soft. Remove to cool on the paper.

3. Tip the remaining oil into the pan to heat. Add the onion. Cook gently for 5 minutes or till softened but not coloured.

4. Add the tomatoes, raisins or sultanas, olives and capers. Season with black pepper. Simmer gently with the lid on for 15 minutes.

5. Add the sugar and vinegar. Simmer for another 15 minutes.

6. Stir the aubergine and celery into the mix. Remove from the heat.

7. Leave the caponata for 30 minutes. Taste and adjust seasoning. Add the parsley and chopped eggs if using. Eat at room temperature.

Red Cabbage with Apple & Spices

Red and purple veg have more health boosters in them than most. But forget that. This has a brilliant colour, plus a mass of spicy, appley, sweet and sour flavours. Try with potato cakes, pork, best bangers and that's just for starters…

Method

1. Preheat oven to 180°C/350°F/gas 4.

2. Strip off and discard the covering leaves of the cabbage. Chop the rest in sections. Cut away the hard core. Discard. Shred the cabbage thinly. Pile into a colander.

3. Prepare the apples and onions, making separate piles. Organize the other ingredients.

4. Get a large casserole dish. Slap a covering layer of cabbage in the bottom. Season it. Layer in a third of the apple then a third of the onion. Add garlic, 1 tablespoon brown sugar and a sprinkling of spice.

5. Repeat till all used. Finish with a layer of cabbage.

6. Season again. Dot the butter over the top. Spoon the vinegar in there.

7. Cover and cook for 1 hour. Check and stir every 20 minutes. Test to see it's the texture you like. Give it extra time if you think it needs it.

For 4

1 red cabbage
2 big cooking apples, peeled, cored and chopped
2 big onions, chopped small
Salt and pepper
3 fat cloves of garlic, crushed
3 tbsps brown sugar
2 tsps mixed spice
25 g/1 oz butter
3 tbsps wine vinegar (try raspberry vinegar)

Eat with:

Mash (pg 22)
Sausages (veggie or otherwise)
Grilled bacon
Sugar-baked bacon (pg 78)
Roast pork (pg 83)
Cheesy potato cakes (pg 94)

why not?

Make red cabbage salad. Shred a load of red cabbage. Slap in a bowl with 1 diced orange, 1 diced apple, 1 sliced avocado, a few crushed walnuts. Make a dressing of mustard, honey, white wine vinegar and sunflower oil topped up with a bit of walnut oil. Toss it together. Tasty.

Vegetable Moussaka

A Greek feast. Layers of soft aubergine and potato in a cinnamon-tinged sauce and creamy topping. Perfect with mezze for big home dinners.

For 4

2 large potatoes, peeled
Olive oil
1 large onion, peeled and finely chopped
3 cloves garlic, crushed
2 x 400 g/14 oz cans chopped tomatoes
A splash of red wine
1 tsp dried or fresh oregano
Pinch of cinnamon
Pinch of sugar
2 tbsps tomato purée
1 x 400 g/14 oz can red kidney beans, drained and rinsed
2 aubergines, sliced
2 tbsps fresh parsley, chopped
Salt and pepper

Topping

20 g/³/₄ oz butter
20 g/³/₄ oz flour
425 ml/³/₄ pint milk
110 g/4 oz Cheddar, grated, plus extra for topping
¹/₂ tsp mustard
1 tbsp lemon juice
Salt and pepper

Eat with:

Tzatziki (pg 140)
Warm pittas
Green salad (pg 140)
Tomato & onion salad (pg 140)
Hummus (pg 140)

Method

1. Boil spuds till just tender. Drain. Slice. Set aside.
2. Heat a bit of oil in a large pan. Cook onion and garlic gently for 5 minutes or till softened, not coloured.
3. Add tomatoes, wine, oregano, cinnamon, sugar and purée. Boil. Reduce heat. Cover. Simmer gently for 10 minutes. Add beans. Simmer another 20 minutes. Taste and season.
4. Meantime, heat 4 tablespoons of oil in a large frying pan. Fry batches of aubergine in a single layer till just soft and golden each side. Remove to wait on kitchen paper. Preheat oven to 190°C/375°F/gas 5.
5. **Topping:** Melt the butter in a small pan over a gentle heat. Add the flour. Stir furiously with a wooden spoon for 2 minutes. Remove from heat. Pour the milk in gradually, beating well with a balloon whisk or spoon as you go to make a smooth thin sauce. Return to the heat.
6. Bring it slowly to the boil, still beating. The sauce will thicken. Add a bit more milk if you think it needs it. Simmer for 2 minutes. Slap in the cheese, mustard, lemon and seasoning. Stir and heat for another minute.
7. **Assembly:** Use 4 small shallow heatproof dishes, or 1 shallow dish approximately 23 x 23 x 6 cm/9 x 9 x 2¹/₂ in deep. Layer the tomato bean mix, aubergine, grated cheese, potato and so on. Finish with aubergines. Leave room to cover with the topping. Sprinkle with extra cheese.
8. Bake for 1 hour or till hot and bubbling. Rest it for 10 minutes before eating.

Courgette, Lemon & Thyme Risotto

Hmm. Risotto can be bland and that doesn't interest me. But this does. Thyme and lemon lift the rice. Courgette gives it a bit of bite. Get someone round to help out and share it.

Method

1. Put the stock into a large pan. Bring to the boil then reduce to a low simmer. Get a ladle ready.

2. In another pan melt butter over a low heat. Add the onion, garlic and thyme. Cook gently for 3–5 minutes without colouring, until soft.

3. Increase heat. Add rice. Stir to coat. Tip in the wine or cider and let it bubble. Stir so it won't stick or burn until half the liquid is gone.

4. Reduce heat. Add 2 ladles of stock. Stir as the rice absorbs it. Add it another couple of ladles and stir again till absorbed. Add the turmeric or saffron.

5. Throw in the courgettes then 2 more ladles of stock and a good squeeze of lemon.

6. Continue watching and stirring until the stock is done and you have a creamy soupy mix. Add more if you need. Don't rush the process – it could take up to 30 minutes. Have music on and take it easy.

7. Throw in a handful of Parmesan. Season with salt and black pepper. Add a knob of butter if you like.

8. Serve in bowls with extra herbs on top and more Parmesan or grate at the table. Eat with watercress and chicory salad.

For 4
1 litre/1¾ pints veg or chicken stock (pg 138)
50 g/2 oz butter
1 medium onion, finely chopped
2 cloves garlic, sliced
2 sprigs fresh thyme
225 g/8 oz Arborio or Vialone Nano risotto rice
100 ml/3½ fl oz white wine or dry cider
Small pinch of turmeric, or a few strands of saffron dissolved in 1 tbsp hot water
275 g/10 oz courgettes in small cubes
Juice of ¼ lemon
Freshly grated Parmesan
Salt and black pepper
Extra butter and herbs (optional)

Watercress & chicory salad
Toss chopped chicory, watercress and shallot into a bowl. Mix with mustard or other dressing (see pg 140 for ideas).

why not?
Use local asparagus instead of courgettes when in season (mid April–late June).

Beans & Peas with Lemon Dressing

For 6–8
450 g/1 lb fresh mixed
  beans & peas, e.g. fine
  green, sugar snap, runner
  beans, shelled peas
2 tbsps chopped parsley
2 shallots, sliced thinly
Lemon dressing
1 tbsp Dijon mustard
Good pinch caster sugar
Juice of 1 lemon
4 tbsps olive oil
3 tbsps sour cream or
  crème fraîche
Pinch of salt
1 tbsp hot water

Eat with:
A banquet of salads.

Beans and peas get all mixed up in a beautiful little lemon sauce. Best homegrown and in season (summer) though the dressing cheers them up any time.

Method
1. Put a large-ish pan one-third full of lightly salted water on to boil.
2. Slide the mix of beans in. With the lid off, boil for 2 minutes.
3. Add the shelled peas. Cook for another 2 or till tender but crisp to the bite still.
4. Meantime, fill a bowl with very cold water. A cube or two of ice would help.
5. Drain the beans and slap them into the ice-cold water to stop the cooking and preserve the colour.
6. Drain well. Blot on kitchen roll if you like. Slap the beans into a bowl.
7. **Lemon dressing:** Stick the dressing ingredients into a jar. Put the lid on and shake well. Alternatively mix in a bowl.
8. Pour the dressing over the beans. Add the parsley and shallots. Mix well. Cool for barbies.

Spinach, Avocado & Bacon Salad

Rock 'n' roll with this simple salad. It's a little bit crunchy … a little bit salty. Toss the lot in a sharp-suited dressing. PS Dressing salad leaves? Coat all over by using your fingers.

For 2
1 tbsp olive oil
4 rashers streaky bacon
2 slices crustless bread, cubed
Avocado, peeled and cubed
Bunch of baby spinach

Method
1. Heat olive oil in a pan. Fry bacon till crisp. Sit on kitchen paper.
2. Fry the cubes of bread in the bacon fat. Drain on the paper.
3. Toss the avocado and spinach in a dressing of your choice (see pg 140 for ideas). Chop up bacon.
4. Add the bacon and croutons, and toss.

why not?
Fizz this up… Slap in cooked green beans and a bit of chopped shallot. Drizzle a bit of pomegranate molasses in there with the dressing.

Brilliant Vegetables

For 3–4

2 tsps sesame oil

1 tbsp sunflower oil

2 cloves garlic, sliced thinly

A little fresh ginger, grated or sliced

200 g/7 oz tenderstem broccoli in 1 cm/½ in slices

4 tbsps stock (pg 138, or use Marigold if no homemade) or water

2 splashes soy sauce

2–3 tbsps oyster sauce

---

variation

CHOICE STIR-FRY
Try with purple sprouting broccoli, sliced pak choi or sliced courgettes.

For 3–4

2–3 tbsps olive oil

2 heads of big broccoli

Sea salt

1 lemon, in wedges

---

variation

HOT BROCCOLI
Sprinkle with a little de-seeded, finely chopped chilli.

Bad press vegetables turned into heroes. Don't judge them. Just try them.

Slim Sesame Broccoli

Tender broccoli sweetens up in oyster sauce. Slice these guys up for an awesome stir-fry.

Method

1. Heat a wok or pan. Add sesame or sunflower oil.

2. When hot, add the garlic and ginger. Turn quickly to prevent burning.

3. After a few seconds, add the broccoli. Toss and turn for 2–3 minutes.

4. Add the stock or water. Turn for another minute or so till just soft with a bit of bite or how you like it. Mix in the soy and oyster sauce.

Fat Broccoli

Tastes a bit like Chinese restaurant seaweed. Get it nice and dry before you fry it.

Method

1. Wash the broccoli. Slice very thinly. Slap on to a tea towel or kitchen paper to dry thoroughly.

2. Heat a lidded sauté pan. Add the olive oil.

3. Tip the broccoli in. Slam the lid on.

4. Cook for 2 minutes or till just browned a bit, softening but crisp still. Turn. Replace lid and cook for another minute.

5. Serve with sea salt and lemon chunks for squeezing.

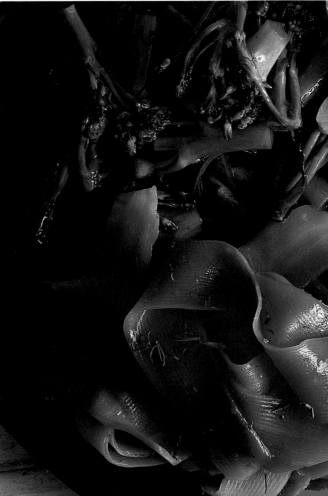

Carrot Pasta

Delicious carroty pasta-lookalike.

Method

1. Bring a bit of water to boil.
2. Meantime, use a potato peeler to cut the carrots into ribbons.
3. Slap the carrots into the boiling water for 20 seconds. Tip into a sieve.
4. Slap butter and sugar to melt in a pan. When hot, toss in the carrots.
5. Stir-fry for 2–3 minutes till just soft. Add the lemon or lime rind, and season. Mix some herb in. Lovely!

Edgy Cumin Cauliflower

Sex up your cauliflower. This veg needs it.

Method

1. Preheat oven to 220°C/425°F/gas 7.
2. Tip the cauli on to a baking tray. Add garlic and drizzle with a little oil.
3. Sprinkle with cumin and salt to taste. Turn to coat.
4. Roast till tender. Delicious hot or cold.

For 3–4
4 carrots, peeled
25 g/1 oz butter
1 flat tbsp caster sugar
Rind of ½ lemon or 1 lime, grated
Salt and black pepper
Sprinkle of thyme or finely chopped sage, parsley or rosemary

why not?
Boil carrots in water with a glug of elderflower cordial for extra sweetness.

For 3–4
1 cauliflower, in small florets
3 cloves garlic, peeled and sliced
Olive oil
Ground cumin
Coarse sea salt

Meat

A ndy's goal-orientated so no surprise he was up for meat. Steak's his meal of choice – Saturdays after the match – in school sometimes off to our friendly neighbourhood butcher then back to the common room for a bit of a grilling. My challenge? Get him to diversify – tackle other kinds of lovely stuff like my roast crunchy duck, sugared bacon, top sausage Yorkshires, lamb korma, lovely lamb koftas plus some of the leaner eats you can do with chicken. Meat's major protein. Eat it to power yourself on. And red meat's great for sharpening the brain – it's the iron. Get yourself loads of veg, salad, carbs with it. Buying your own meat? Try to get free-range and local if you can. Proper butchers know how to treat it so you'll get more interesting cuts and a better flavour. Andy's family get theirs from the farm shop. Cook it in a variety of ways – roasting, grilling, baking, boiling, griddling. Occasionally fry it but if you want to stay on the ball you want to keep the fat down.

Top Sausage Yorkshires

Makes 8
4 eggs
300 ml/¹/₂ pint milk
225 g/8 oz flour
Salt and pepper
8 best organic chipolatas
Sunflower or light olive oil

variations

BACON & HERB
At STEP 3 stretch 4 slices of streaky bacon until thin. Cut in half. Wrap each half around a chipolata. Tuck a sprig of rosemary between the banger and bacon if you like.

VEGETARIAN
At STEP 5 lightly fry vegetarian sausages or throw in some roasted butternut squash and red onion.

CLASSIC TOAD IN THE HOLE
At STEP 3 put 6–8 large quality sausages into a Yorkshire pudding tin (mine is 30 x 20 x 7 cm/ 12 x 8 x 3 in) with a bit of oil. Bake for 6 minutes. At STEP 6 while the oil in the tin is still very hot, pour the batter mix over it. Cook for 20–40 mins.

why not?

Try using big sausages. Or make plain without sausages.

Classic Toad-in-the-Hole but easier and speedier. Crispy, golden and packed with bangers. Slap in the oven after the match. Team with creamy mash, onion relish, homestyle ketchup.

Method

1. Preheat oven to 230°C/450°F/gas 8.
2. **Start batter:** Whisk eggs and milk together with a pinch of salt using an electric mixer (whisk attachment) or by hand with a balloon or electric hand whisk to look like milkshake. Leave for 20 minutes.
3. Sit bangers on a baking tray. Bake for 5 minutes.
4. Drizzle a bit of oil into each hole of two four-hole individual Yorkshire pud tins. Put in the oven to preheat. The hotter they are, the higher the rising.
5. **Finish batter:** Sift flour and pepper into the milk. Whisk furiously by hand or machine. Tip into a measuring jug.
6. Remove sizzling tins from the oven. Sit a banger in each hole. Pour batter in right up to rims.
7. Slide tins carefully back onto middle shelf to rise. Cook without opening the door for 20 mins till high and golden.

Lamb Korma & Cucumber Salad

Every week the lads head off for a curry or sort an awesome one at home. Korma's a brilliant match of spices, almonds and yogurt that loves lamb and doesn't bang out the heat. Give it a trial with cooling cucumber salad.

Method

1. Slap lamb in a bowl with half the yogurt. Mix to coat.
2. Tip onion, chilli, garlic, ginger, almonds, korma paste, half the coriander and the water into a blender or processor. Blitz to a fine paste. (By hand: chop fine and stir in the water.)
3. Tip oil into a large pan or casserole over low heat. Add paste. Stir for 1 minute to stop it sticking as it thickens.
4. Chuck the lamb in with salt and lemon juice. Mix well.
5. Increase heat to bring curry to a gentle boil, stirring.
6. Reduce to a very low heat. Cook, covered, for 1 hour. Occasionally check. Add a splash of water if it gets too dry, but you want a thick sauce.
7. Add remaining yogurt. Cook for a further 30–40 minutes. Taste. Adjust seasoning, adding more juice or yogurt.
8. You can cook this in the oven at 200°C/400°F/gas 6 for 20 minutes, then lower heat slightly for 1 hour or till tender.
9. Make cucumber salad. Enjoy.

For 4
2 lbs cubed lamb (leg or shoulder)
4 tbsps plain yogurt
2 onions, chopped
2 chillies, de-seeded and chopped
2 cloves garlic, chopped
2^1/$_2$ cm/1 in piece of ginger, peeled and grated
50 g/2 oz ground almonds
4 tbsps korma paste
Handful fresh coriander
100 ml/3^1/$_2$ oz water
2 tbsps groundnut or sunflower oil
Pinch of salt
Squeeze of lemon juice

Eat with:
Poppadoms
Warm naan bread
Mango chutney

Cucumber salad
1 cucumber
1 tsp salt
1 tbsp plain yogurt
2 tbsps coconut cream
1 clove garlic, crushed
1–2 chillies, de-seeded and finely sliced
1 small onion, thinly sliced
2 tbsps lime juice

Peel cucumber and slice it in half lengthways. Whip the seeds out with a teaspoon. Cut the flesh across in thin half moon shapes. Sprinkle with the salt and leave for 30 mins. Rinse and dry. Combine all other salad ingredients. Mix in cucumber.

why not?

Make korma a day or two ahead to save time and develop flavour.

Old Fashioned Sugared Bacon

For 6

2 kg/4½ lbs bacon joint, ham or gammon
2 bay leaves
Peeled onion
8 black peppercorns
2 tbsps black treacle, maple syrup or demarara sugar
Whole cloves

Glaze

6 oz demarara sugar
2½ cm/1 in piece peeled ginger, grated
2 tbsps English mustard
Juice of 1 lemon
3 tbsps apple juice or water

Pease pudding

225 g/8 oz yellow split peas
1 small carrot, chopped
1 small onion, chopped
2 cloves garlic, crushed
1 bay leaf
Stock from bacon or water
Butter
Salt and pepper
Grated nutmeg

Eat with:

Mash (pg 22)
Baked spuds (pg 98)
Roasties
Crunchy Herb Spuds (pg 99)
Red cabbage (pg 67)
Coleslaw (pg 141)
Orange salad (pg 140)
Potato salad (pg 96)
Apple sauce (pg 138)

If you're a bacon or gammon fan you'll love this. The sugar glaze packs the meat with taste and looks magnificent. Eat some hot. Save the rest for salads, sarnies and teaming up with other stuff. One bit of cooking makes a week of top eating.

Method

1. **Day or two before:** Tie joint with string like a parcel to keep it together. Put it into a large bowl. Cover with cold water to draw out salt. Fridge it. Soak split peas in cold water overnight.

2. **On the day:** Drain. Put meat into a very large pan or casserole. Cover with fresh water. Add bay leaves, onion, peppercorns and black treacle or syrup or sugar.

3. Sit pan on a low heat. Bring to the boil very slowly (could take 30 minutes).

4. Reduce heat, simmer gently for 45 minutes then remove.

5. **Glaze:** Whisk all ingredients together in a pan over a low heat with a balloon whisk. Boil for a few minutes to reduce to a syrup. Set aside.

6. Preheat oven to 200°C/400°F/gas 6.

7. Drain meat over a bowl (save liquid for stock). Chuck out onion etc.

8. Sit meat on a board. Cut skin away from top leaving the fat. Score a criss-cross pattern across but don't cut the string. Stick whole cloves in.

9. Sit meat in a roasting tin. Brush with glaze. Cook for 30–45 minutes. Re-glaze 4 times to flavour and colour. Rest meat for at least 10 minutes before carving.

10. **Pease pudding:** Drain soaked peas. Slap in a pan with the carrot, onion, garlic, bay leaf and stock or water. Boil fiercely for at least 10 minutes. Cover. Simmer over a low heat for 1–1½ hours till tender. Drain. Bash up with butter, seasoning and nutmeg using a masher.

Crunchy Chicken Strippers

For 4
4 good chicken breasts
Butter and oil for frying
Plain white flour for coating
3 good pinches chilli powder
Salt and black pepper
1–2 eggs, beaten
Polenta (plain or with bits
   of dried vegetable)

Dips
Sweet chilli sauce
Mustard or harissa mayo
   (pg 139)
Ketchup (pg 139)

Salsa Verde
Blitz 3 crushed garlic cloves, 1 bunch torn parsley, 1 bunch torn basil, 1½ tbsps rinsed capers, 1 tbsp Dijon mustard and 1 tbsp white wine vinegar in a processor. Add 6–8 tbsps extra virgin olive oil drizzled very slowly through a funnel, till you get a mayo-style mix. Store in the fridge and stir before serving.

why not?
Make Chicken & Chips in a Basket. Scrunch kitchen paper up to line some bowls. Make up a batch of my oven baked big chips (pg 32) and slap them into the paper. Bang the cooked strippers on top. Eat with your fingers and salt, ketchup and malt vinegar. Great for parties and gatherings. Lovely anytime.

Get your mates working out on these. They're tasty. Polenta gets chicken excellently crunchy. Perfect for supper with dips and big chips. Prep loads ahead to whack into baskets for party-style munchies.

Method
1. Make salsa verde.
2. Preheat oven to 200°C/400°F/gas 6. Flatten chicken fillets. Lay on a board between clingfilm. Bash with flat of hand or rolling pin.
3. Cut chicken into slices – at least 8 cm/3 in or longer.
4. **To coat:** Slap flour, chilli powder and seasoning onto one large plate. Put beaten eggs on a second. Spread polenta onto a third. Coat slices in flour then egg then polenta. Sit on a baking tray.
5. Cook for 10 minutes till white all through (stick a knife in to check). Or fry for 2–3 minutes each side in a little butter and oil till done.
6. Eat with chips, salsa verde, other dips and salads.

Lime Sherbet Chicken

I adore this. I've almost eaten it too often it's so addictive. Marinate the chicken in the fridge overnight to maximize taste and save time. It's light (good for health and weight) and packed with useful protein. Good for a training boost.

Method

1. Flatten the chicken a bit. **Either:** Place on a board and thump with the flat of your hand. **Or:** Lay between clingfilm. Bash with a rolling pin.
2. Mix the ginger, lime rind and juice, garlic, coriander and a good glug of olive oil. Save half for a dressing.
3. Tip the rest into a shallow dish. Add in the chicken. Rub it in the marinade. Leave for at least 30 minutes but longer if you like. Wash your hands well after handling raw chicken.
4. Put a lightly oiled griddle pan on to heat. Slap the chicken on to sizzle. Turn when the first side is browned. Cook the other side. Turn again if you need. Cooking time will vary depending on thickness of the meat and degree of heat. Each fillet should be cooked (white) through but still moist. Test it with a knife to check. Season with sea salt.
5. Serve the chicken in one piece or cut into diagonals. Add a bit more oil to the reserved dressing and drizzle it all over. Sit on rice or couscous. Also great with crispy herbed spuds. Salad. Griddled veg, e.g. courgettes, aubergine, butternut squash (sliced, brushed with oil, seared on a griddle). Tasty!

For 4
4 skinless chicken breasts
Marinade
5 cm/2 in piece ginger, peeled and grated
Rind of 2 plump limes and juice of 4 plump limes
1 clove garlic, crushed
3 tbsps coriander, finely chopped
Olive oil
Sea salt

variations
LIME KEBABS
At STEP 1 leave the chicken unflattened. Cut it into chunks. At STEP 4 preheat a grill. Thread the chicken onto metal skewers or wooden ones soaked in cold water for 20 minutes. Grill, turning till done. Serve with griddled veg.
VEGGIE
Use Quorn and tofu instead of chicken.
THAI CHICKEN FINGERS
At STEP 1 cut the chicken into thin finger-length strips. At STEP 2 put the dressing ingredients into a blender adding 1 chopped red chilli. Use lemons instead of limes and mint instead of coriander if you like. At STEP 4 griddle the chicken fingers till cooked through. Spicy. Delicious.

why not?
Chop lime chicken into a wrap or salad box for a lean eat or snack. Great slapped on a salad bowl.

Roast Pork with Apples & Trimmings

This one's asking to be Sunday lunch, though it's easy enough to work it midweek. Chuck your apples in to bake with the meat. It flavours up the spuds. Sorts a nice fruity gravy.

Method

1. Boil spuds in a large pan of lightly salted water for 5–10 minutes till just softening. Drain well. Set aside.

2. Preheat oven to 200°C/400°F/gas 6.

3. Score rind. Cut close parallel lines across skin on the meat with a sharp knife (leave any string intact).

4. Rub sea salt well into the lines and the top. Stick herb sprigs in.

5. Put a good glug of oil in a large roasting tin. Sit the meat in there. Roast for 10 minutes then stick spuds in – turning in sizzling fat. Roast for another 10 minutes.

6. Reduce heat to 190°C/375°F/gas 5. Sit apples cut side down in the tin with the garlic cloves.

7. Cook till done. (Depends on joint size. Test by poking with a skewer. Juices should run clear and meat should be cooked through.) Rest in a warm place. Remove apples and garlic while still holding shape – not pulpy.

8. Increase the heat to 220°C/425°F/gas 7. Move pan up a shelf to crisp the spuds. Remove and keep warm when done.

9. Gravy: Add a bit of water to the appley juices in the tin. Scrape any bits off with a wooden spoon. Stir over the hob to boil.

10. Carve meat. Give everyone roasties, apple, garlic and gravy.

For 4
4 large potatoes (Maris Pipers or King Edwards are good), peeled and quartered
1 small loin of pork joint
Coarse sea salt
4–6 bits rosemary or sage
Olive or sunflower oil
2 sharp eating apples, halved
6–8 cloves garlic

Eat with:
Green bean spaghetti (pg 53)
Baked cauliflower (pg 73)
Carrot pasta (pg 73)

variation
TOP CRACKLING
Preheat oven to 220°C/425°F/gas 7. Cut skin off pork with sharp knife. Sit on baking paper in tin. Salt it. Roast for 40 minutes or till crisp. Keep warm. Reduce heat to 200°C/400°F/gas 6. Smear honey and mustard mix over fat on pork joint. Roast as recipe. Eat with crackling.

why not?
Make yourself a lovely hot pork roll. Slap a slice between bread with mustard and warm apple sauce. Or try it cold with apple sauce, mustard mayo (pg 139), rocket and coleslaw.

Perfect Beef Stir-Fry

For 2–3
Marinade
450 g/1 lb rump or
  sirloin steak
3 cloves garlic, peeled
  and finely chopped
1 tsp coriander, finely
  chopped
2 tbsps soy sauce
1 tbsp rice wine
2 tsps caster sugar
1 tbsp cornflour
Rice
150 g/5 oz basmati rice
300 ml/10 fl oz cold water
Sauce
2 tbsps soy sauce
1½ tsps sugar
Squeeze of lime (optional)
Dash of sesame oil
Stir-fry
2 tbsps sunflower oil
1 tsp sesame oil
6 spring onions, chopped
  lengthways

variations
DUCK STIR-FRY
Use sliced duck
breasts (fat removed)
instead of beef.
VEGGIE STIR-FRY
Use mushrooms
or tofu.

Stir-fries can be a bit average, a bit bitty, but I've never complained about this one. All the oriental flavours complement each other beautifully to produce a really cracking beef stir-fry.

Method
1. Beef: Cut into thin diagonal slices across grain (pattern). Slice into bite-sized bits.
2. Slap in a bowl with garlic, coriander, soy, rice wine, sugar and cornflour. Marinade for 30 mins or more (fridge overnight if you'd like).
3. Rice: Wash rice in sieve under tap. Add to a pan with the water. Bring to the boil. Cover. Simmer on low heat for 10 minutes or till water is absorbed. Remove. Let it stand.
4. Sauce: Meantime mix soy, sugar, lime if using and sesame oil.
5. Stir-fry: Heat wok or deep frying pan. Add sunflower and sesame oils. Chuck in half the beef. Stir-fry for 1–2 minutes using a long-handled wooden spoon till just browned. (Don't overcook. Goes leathery.) Remove. Keep warm. Repeat with rest of beef. Remove.
6. Stir-fry spring onions for 1 minute. Slap beef back in to reheat. Add sauce. Stir well to heat through.
7. Drain rice. Fluff with fork. Stuff into bowls. Top with stir-fry.

Steak Jalapeño Mojos

These can be absolutely packed and massive, as I found out to my messy delight – bits of marinated steak and filling flying everywhere. Or trim and neat. Your choice.

Method

1. Marinade: Smash garlic, peppers, coriander, salt and pepper together with a pestle and mortar. Tip into a jar. Add lime and lemon juices, vinegar and oil. Screw the lid on and shake.

2. Meat: Slap steaks into a shallow dish. Tip marinade over. Rub in well. Chill for at least 1 hour. Return to room temp before cooking.

3. Fillings: Prep just before cooking. Sit avocado stone in guacamole to keep it pretty.

4. Get your griddle or frying pan well hot. Slap steaks on. Cook for 2 minutes per side or till done as you like. Beef's best still pink inside. Rest meat somewhere warm.

5. Warm tortillas in a frying pan or oven till soft.

6. Carve meat into thin diagonals. Chuck into tortillas with fillings.

For 4
4 rump or sirloin steaks
8 corn tortilla wraps
Marinade
4 cloves garlic, peeled
   and crushed
4–6 bits pickled jalapeño
   peppers
2 tbsps coriander
Sea salt and black pepper
Juice of 2 limes
Juice of 1 lemon
1 tbsp white wine vinegar
2 tbsps olive oil
Fillings
Guacamole (pg 140)
Sour cream
Chopped tomato or salsa
   (pg 139)
Iceberg or other crisp
   lettuce
Chopped red onion
Grated Cheddar or
   crumbled Lancashire

variation
CHICKEN MOJOS
At STEP 2 flatten 4 chicken fillets with a rolling pin. Slap them into the marinade. At STEP 4 cook for 5 minutes each side or till white and tender. Eat hot as above or cold in a wrap, salad or sandwich.

Whole Roast Crunchy Duck

For 3–4
1 duck, approx 2.75 kg/6 lbs
Sea salt and pepper

Cherry sauce:
Slap 3–4 tbsps cherry jam
into a pan with 150 ml/
¼ pint red wine or
pomegranate juice. Whisk.
Simmer gently for 5 mins.

Marmalade sauce:
Whack 3–4 tbsps
marmalade into a pan with
the juice of a large orange
or 150 ml/¼ pint orange
juice or ginger wine. Whisk.
Simmer gently for 5 mins.

Eat with:
Spuds roasted in duck fat
Boiled baby spuds rolled
in parsley or mint, butter,
salt, lemon and black pepper
Watercress

why not?
Use leftover duck
for a pack-up wrap.
Shred and mix with
matchstick-cut
cucumber, spring
onion, and a bit of
cherry jam or
hoisin sauce.

I've been known to polish off a whole half a duck myself.
This is a top family favourite. It's so easy, and well
impressive. Serve with a fruity sauce to lift the taste. Save
the fat for roasting potatoes.

Method
1. Preheat oven to 220°C/425°F/gas 7.
2. Dry duck with kitchen roll (dry means crispy).
3. Sit it on a rack in a roasting tin.
4. Prick all over with a fork. Rub in sea salt and pepper.
5. Roast for 25 minutes. Pour fat off carefully into a bowl.
6. Decrease temperature to 180°C/350°F/gas 4.
7. Leave duck to cook for 2 hours. Carefully pour off the fat every
30 mins or so.
8. Meantime make your sauce of choice.
9. Let duck rest for 5 minutes when it's done (deep golden brown, salty and crispy).
10. Cut into 4 with a sharp knife, kitchen shears or scissors. Cut along the back to get it in half then just above the leg to quarter it. Plate it. Tip the sauce over it.

Sweet 5-spice Duck Legs

A personal favourite. I love my duck to have a crispy skin and the 5-spice adds the cool Asian flavour. The sauce is essential. Rest these guys on a pile of fried potatoes and enjoy with a mountain of salad. Makes a great treat or impress someone special.

Method

1. Preheat oven to 200°C/400°F/gas 6.
2. Chuck the duck legs into a roasting tin or dish big enough to take them in a single layer. Poke the rosemary and garlic cloves underneath.
3. Prick the legs all over with a fork. Rub a mix of 5-spice and sea salt well into the skin. Bake for 1 hour. Pour fat off carefully once or twice.
4. Meantime, melt the redcurrant jelly with the wine or juice and water in a small pan. Use a balloon whisk to break up the jelly. Simmer it for 5 minutes or till well amalgamated. Remove from the heat.
5. Remove duck. Pour off remaining fat. Tip liquid jelly over meat. Roast for another 15 minutes. Cracking.

For 4
4 duck legs
2 sprigs rosemary
4 cloves garlic, peeled
1–2 tsps Chinese 5-spice powder
1–2 tsps sea salt
2 tbsps redcurrant jelly or morello cherry jam
150 ml/$\frac{1}{4}$ pint red wine or apple or pomegranate juice
4 tbsps water

Eat with:
Crunchy Herb Spuds (pg 99) or mash (pg 22)
Green bean spaghetti (pg 53) or peas
Griddled butternut squash

why not?

Try roast sherbet duck breast. Fry duck breast fillets till brown each side. Roast on a rack at 220°C/425°F/gas 7 for 10 minutes or till done as you like. Rest for 3 mins. Slice diagonally. Drizzle with a little pomegranate juice and molasses. It fizzes...

Homestyle Hotdogs

Makes 6–8

700 g/1½ lbs pork steak, shoulder, belly or best pork mince
2–3 tsps fennel seeds
40 g/1½ oz white breadcrumbs
3 cloves garlic, crushed
1–2 red chillies, de-seeded and finely chopped
3 spring onions
Grated lemon rind
Salt and black pepper
Olive oil for cooking

Relish

1 tbsp olive oil
1 tbsp butter
2 big red onions, thinly sliced
½–1 tbsp brown sugar
2 tbsps balsamic vinegar

variations

HOMESTYLE PORK BURGERS

At STEP 1 blitz coarser mince than for bangers. At STEP 6 mould into burger shapes. At STEP 7 fry or grill the burgers. At STEP 9 stack with tomato, rocket, sliced Gruyère and griddled apple or pineapple.

PORK & FENNEL MEATBALLS

At STEP 6 roll the mix into meatballs. Fry to colour. Sit the balls in my tomato ginger sauce (pg 52). Simmer gently in a covered pan for 10–15 minutes or till cooked through. Sit on a heap of spaghetti or penne. Sprinkle with Parmesan.

why not?

Skip the bread. Enjoy with mash 'n' onion gravy, or slap 'em on couscous.

Way healthier than bought hotdogs, these also taste so much better – which has to be a winning combo. Fennel's a great flavourer of pork but use your own herb or spice if you like. You've got to try the sweet onion relish – it's brilliant.

Method

1. Own mince: Cut meat in cubes. Blitz a few at a time in a processor for coarse sausage-meat style paste. **Bought mince:** Blitz mince in a processor to make it pastier.

2. Crush fennel roughly in a pestle and mortar for bits, or blitz to powder in a spice or coffee grinder.

3. Slap mince, breadcrumbs, fennel, garlic, chilli, finely chopped spring onion, lemon rind and seasoning into a bowl. Mix with your hands, squeezing ingredients together. Chill for 30 minutes or more.

4. Relish: Heat oil and butter in a pan. Cook onion over a very low heat for 10 minutes till softened but not coloured.

5. Stir in sugar and vinegar. Cook gently for 20 minutes till sticky and jam-like.

6. Hotdogs: Shape mix into 6–8 sausages, squeezing together. Brush with a bit of olive oil.

7. Heat a bit of oil in a frying pan. Fry sausages gently on all sides. If a bit breaks off, don't panic. Cook all through.

8. Oven cook? Fry to brown all sides then cook at 200°C/400°F/gas 6 for 10 minutes or till cooked through.

9. Assemble: Slap into roll or baguette with onion relish, ketchup (pg 139), mustard and salad leaves. Great with baked sweet potato chips (pg 32).

Lovely Lamb Koftas

Makes 8
700 g/1 1/2 lbs minced lamb
2 small onions, grated
4 cloves garlic, crushed
1 tsp allspice
1/2 tsp ground cumin
1/4 tsp sweet paprika
1 tsp dried chilli flakes
3 tbsps chopped flatleaf
  parsley
Salt and black pepper
Sunflower oil for brushing

Baba Ganoush
Preheat oven to 200°C/
400°F/gas 6. Roast 2
aubergines on a baking tray
till skin blackens and flesh
softens (30–45 minutes).
Cool. Peel skin away. Drain
in sieve or colander for 30
minutes. Blitz in a blender
or processor with 2
crushed garlic cloves. Mix
in 2 tbsps tahini, 3 tbsps
lemon juice, 1/2 tsp ground
cumin and sea salt to taste.
Sprinkle with chopped
parsley and chill.

variation
KOFTA POCKETS
At STEP 1 cover 150 g/
5 oz bulgar wheat with
boiling water. Soak for
30 minutes. Drain and
dry. At STEP 2 add the
dried soaked wheat to
the lamb mix. At STEP
3 divide into burger
shapes but do not
squeeze. At STEP 6
cook in a pan for 4
minutes each side or
till cooked through.
Slap in a pitta with
hummus, garlic, tzatziki
and salad.

Juicy lamb on sticks with loads of warm spices. Get the best mince or mince your own lamb shoulder or steak in a processor. Wraparound kebabs basically. Team with baba ganoush and mezze.

Method
1. If using wooden skewers, soak them in cold water for 20 minutes before you want to cook.
2. Slap the lamb into a bowl with the grated onion, garlic, spices, chilli, parsley and seasoning. Add a splash of water to bind.
3. Mix together with your hands squeezing the components together into a smooth paste. Divide the paste into 8 fat sausage shapes.
4. Chill for later, or if cooking now, preheat the grill or griddle.
5. Take a metal or wooden skewer. Thread a sausage then elongate and mould it around the skewer for a thinner sausage. Repeat.
6. Brush each sausage with a little oil. Grill or griddle the meat, turning as you go till cooked through (5–10 minutes). Serve with baba ganoush. Warm pittas. Tzatziki. Hummus. Rice or couscous. Tomato & onion salad.

Chicken in a Paper Bag

For very little effort you get a brilliant Chinese meal. Baking it in the bag makes the meat extra tender.

Method
1. Marinade: Mix the hoisin sauce, garlic (if using) cooking wine and oil in a bowl. Chuck in the chicken. Mix well. Leave for at least 30 mins.
2. Add the spring onion. Preheat oven to 200°C/400°F/gas 6.
3. Cut out two large squares of greaseproof paper. Divide the chicken mix between them sitting it in a single layer. Make two parcels. Scrunch or fold the paper up around the meat, leaving room for the steam to rise but enclosing the meat. Sit the parcels on a baking tray. Cook for 20 minutes.
4. Rice: Meantime, prepare your rice. Wash in a sieve under the tap. Slap in a pan with the water. Bring to the boil. Cover. Simmer on a low heat for 10 mins or till the water's absorbed. Take from the heat and let it stand.
5. Stir-fry: Heat a wok and add the oils. Add the garlic and spring onion and fry till soft. Chuck in the ginger if using and pak choi. Stir-fry till tender. Add the soy, rice wine and sugar. Heat through.
6. Test chicken is cooked. Use a knife to check it's all white (no pink).
7. Drain and fluff the rice with a fork. Serve in bowls with stir-fry and top with chicken.

For 2
Marinade
2–3 tbsps hoisin sauce
1 clove garlic, crushed (optional)
A little Chinese cooking wine
Drizzle sesame oil
2 spring onions, sliced

2 good size quality chicken breasts, in bite-sized pieces

75 g/3 oz rice
150 ml/5 fl oz cold water

Stir-fry
2 tsps sesame oil
1 tbsp sunflower oil
2 cloves garlic, crushed
2–3 gratings fresh ginger (optional)
1 bunch spring onion, chopped
3 bunches pak choi, chopped
Splash soy sauce
Splash Chinese rice wine
Good pinch of sugar

why not?
Unwrap parcels. Tip onto a bed of stir-fried noodles and pak choi.

Potatoes

Liv's passionate about spuds. Weird I know but I'm with her all the way. There's nothing like a properly cooked potato. Picking the right type is particularly important for cooking. You've got to cast them correctly. Floury characters (King Edward, Maris Piper) are real heroes and like to be mashed (Liv's favourite), bashed, piped, roasted, fried, chipped, smashed up for potato cakes. Waxy salad geezers prefer sharp action. Slicing and chopping for salads, hash, bravas, frittatas. Don't imagine that potatoes are just there for their carbs by the way. You can turn that beautiful energy into really cool food like damned fine potato pancakes to dish up with homecured salmon. Liv round for dinner? Whip up sweet potato gnocchi. Favourites like old school Cornish pasties and luscious shepherd's pie rely on good winter potatoes. Summertime get new ones – light and lovely with a bit of butter, seasoning, fresh herb and lemon. OK, growers break all the rules so you get new potatoes at Christmas – but they don't look right at the top of the tree. Spuds are like home. Get yourself a plate when you're back from the movies…

Neat Potato Cakes

Makes 8
700 g/1 1/2 lbs floury
   potatoes, peeled
2 tbsps butter
1 egg yolk
1 tsp mustard
Squeeze lemon juice
Salt and black pepper
Plain flour for coating
Olive or sunflower oil and
   butter or duck fat

Eat with:
Bangers – good ones
baked in the oven till
brown and cooked through
Fish – a pile of roughly
chopped smoked salmon,
cherry tomato, dill and
olives in a bit of sour cream
and horseradish
Eggs – fried in olive oil
Bacon – crisply grilled
Ham – cold sliced

variations
At STEP 4 add for:
FISH CAKES
Flaked cooked salmon
BACON CAKES
Crisply cooked bacon
CHEESE CAKES
Handful of grated
Cheddar or Gruyère
MUSHROOM CAKES
Lightly fried mushrooms
BUBBLE & SQUEAK
Cooked bacon and
shredded cabbage
HERB CAKES
Finely chopped dill,
parsley or coriander

They're not posh, but so what? Potato cakes work brilliantly alongside other food favourites (sausages, steaks, fish, veggie stews) and easily adapt to star on their own (fish cakes, bacon cakes, cheese cakes). Season well to maximize flavour.

Method
1. Bring a large pan of lightly salted water to the boil.
2. Cut the potatoes into large chunks. Boil until just tender.
3. Drain. Slap back into the warm pan. Jiggle for 1 minute to dry.
4. Mash well with a fork or masher. Add the butter, egg yolk, mustard, lemon juice and seasoning. Beat together till stiffly creamy.
5. Scatter the flour over a large plate. Season lightly.
6. Flour your hands a bit. Divide the mash and shape into

8 flattish cakes. Dip each one into the flour, shaking off excess. Chill, or cook now.
7. Heat oil and butter or duck fat till well hot in a large pan. **Either:** Fry cakes for 5 mins each side till hot through and golden (don't shift too soon or they stick). **Or:** Sit on a baking tray for 10–15 mins at 190°C/375°F/gas 5. Turn. Bake for another 10 till crisp and tempting.

Sweet Potato Gnocchi

Italian dumplings or Chinese dim sum? These guys have elements of both (it's the ginger). A perfect dish for a date-style dinner.

Method

1. Preheat oven to 200°C/400°F/gas 6.

2. Wash potatoes. Prick with a fork. Slap on a baking tray in oven for 40–60 minutes or till tender. Remove. Slice in half. Cool for 2 minutes.

3. Scoop flesh out into a clean tea towel or bit of muslin. Twist to enclose it. Squeeze to remove excess moisture. Scrape into a bowl.

4. Add the ginger, seasoning, egg yolk and Parmesan. Sift in the flour. Mix together with a fork and fingers for a soft warm dough but handle very lightly.

5. Cut into 4 on a lightly floured board. Cover 3 with a cloth. Roll the first piece into a long thin sausage. Cut into 10. Cover. Repeat.

6. Put a large pan of lightly salted water to boil. Slip gnocchi carefully in. Boil for 2 minutes or till they rise. Remove with a slotted spoon. Drain. Slap into a bowl with a tiny bit of olive oil. Keep warm while cooking others.

7. Sauce: Melt butter in a small pan. Add garlic, lemon and herbs. Pour over gnocchi.

For 3–4

350 g/12 oz sweet potato in skins
Small piece of peeled fresh ginger, very finely grated
Salt and black pepper
1 egg yolk
1 tbsp Parmesan, grated
150 g/5 oz plain white flour
Olive oil

Sauce

50 g/2 oz butter
2 cloves garlic, crushed
Good squeeze of lemon juice
Any herbs

Eat with:

Warm bread to mop up juices
Rocket
Freshly grated Parmesan

Two Mean Potato Salads

For 4
700 g/1½ lbs old
    potatoes, peeled, or
    new potatoes, unpeeled,
    chopped into large
    chunks
4–6 cloves garlic with
    skins left on
2–3 tbsps home mayo or
    good bought one
2–3 tbsps natural yogurt
    or sour cream
Squeeze of lemon juice
Fresh parsley, dill or
    coriander, finely chopped
Salt and black pepper

---

variation
TANGY POTATO
SALAD
At STEP 3 add slices
of red onion, chopped
baby gherkin and
cherry tomatoes.

For 4
700 g/1½ lbs old potatoes,
    peeled, or new potatoes,
    unpeeled, chopped into
    large chunks
4 tbsps home mayo or
    good bought one
1–1½ tbsps Chinese wine
    vinegar
2 drops sesame oil
1 clove garlic, crushed
1–2 tsps horseradish sauce
Squeeze of lemon
Parsley, thyme or coriander
Salt and pepper
4 spring onions, sliced
6 radishes, finely chopped
½ cucumber, finely sliced
75 g/3 oz ham, shredded
English cress

Creamy Garlic

Mix and match with other salads…

Method

1. Boil spuds and garlic in lightly salted water till just tender (test with a knife). If using old floury ones watch they don't disintegrate.
2. Drain. Separate spuds from garlic. Cool them a bit.
3. Remove garlic from skins. Smush the flesh in a bowl. Mix in mayo, yogurt or sour cream. Add lemon juice, herbs and seasoning.
4. Mix into spuds. Team with any salad – cold meats – tarts.

East Meets West

One cultural shock of a fancy salad…

Method

1. Boil potatoes in lightly salted water till just tender. Drain and set aside.
2. Meantime, mix the mayo, vinegar, sesame oil, garlic, horseradish, lemon juice, herb and seasoning. Stir in the spring onions.
3. When the potatoes are just warm, stir in mayo mix.
4. Add most of the radish, cucumber and half the ham. Top with remainder and sprinkle cress over it.
5. Cool it. Eat it.

For 4
4 large baking potatoes
Sunflower or olive oil
(optional)
Salt and black pepper
Butter
Lemon juice

variations

GARLIC BUTTER
Mix 2 tbsps of soft butter with 1 clove crushed garlic, salt and pepper. Slice baked spuds in two. Dab a bit of garlic butter over the top of each. Finish under a hot grill till bubbling.

CRUNCHY MUSTARD
Top baked halved spuds with a mix of mustard and garlic breadcrumbs (pg 47) before grilling.

FILLED SKINS
Bake left over or scooped out skins. Brush insides with butter and seasoning. Add cheese. Heat in the hottest oven for 10 minutes or till crisp. Fill with salads and guacamole or dip in sour cream mixed with dill and crushed garlic.

ROAST BAKERS
At STEP 6 chop hot baked spuds into large chunks. Slap in a roasting tin. Increase oven heat to max. Drizzle with a bit of olive oil, salt and pepper or paprika. Roast for 15 minutes.

Banging Baked Potatoes

What can I say? Liv's favourite bakers…

Method
1. Preheat oven to 200°C/400°F/gas 6.
2. Scrub spuds. Sit on baking tray. Prick with a fork or stick metal skewers through each (cuts cooking time).
3. **Crisp finishers:** Rub skins with a bit of oil and salt.
4. **Softies:** Wrap in foil or bake as is.
5. Cook for 1 hour or till tender.
6. **Serving:** Slice in two or cut a cross in the top. Mash in your butter, lemon juice, salt and pepper and/or slap on a topping.
Italian: Ragu (pg 55), grated Parmesan.
Spicy: Veggie chilli (pg 65), sour cream, grated Cheddar.
Chic: Sour cream and chives with rocket, cherry tomatoes, watercress.
Classic: Shredded ham, chopped apple, dates, celery, garlic in sour cream or mayo.
Greek: Diced Feta, cucumber, tomatoes, black olives.
Tex-Mex: Guacamole, grated Cheddar, sour cream, salsa (pg 139).

Crunchy Herb Spuds & French Chicken

Get these slow roast garlic spuds into your repertoire. Winners on their own or with just about anything. Love 'em. A luxurious dish to impress our Liv with…

Method

1. Potatoes: Preheat oven to 220°C/425°F/gas 7.

2. Cut the potatoes into bite-sized chunks. Slap them into a non-stick roasting tin with the garlic and finely chopped herbs. Drizzle with olive oil. Turn to coat. Roast for 50–60 minutes or till crisp outside, tender in the middle. Turn once or twice during cooking.

3. Chicken: 20 minutes before the spuds are done put the chicken between 2 layers of clingfilm. Flatten by bashing with a rolling pin. Don't bother if your fillets are already thin.

4. Tip the flour onto a large plate. Season it. Sit the chicken in and turn to coat well.

5. Put the oil and butter into a large heavy-bottomed frying pan. Heat till it starts to brown but don't let it burn. Add the chicken. Cook for 3–4 minutes or till the bottom browns (check). Turn.

6. Fry for another 5–6 minutes or till cooked right through (white, not pink). Test by cutting the fattest. Remove and keep warm.

7. Sauce: Pour the wine, juice or stock into the pan. Stir well to incorporate all the pan bits and juices where the flavour sits. Boil up for 2–3 minutes till it reduces a bit. Add in the mustard and crème fraîche. Stir. Let it bubble for another 3 minutes.

8. Season the sauce. Pour over the chicken. Sprinkle with herbs. Serve with crunchy potatoes and great bread to mop up the juices. Classic.

For 4

Potatoes
4 baking potatoes, peeled
8 cloves garlic, chopped
3 sprigs rosemary
Olive oil

Chicken
4 chicken breasts
Flour for coating
Salt and black pepper
1 tbsp olive oil
1 tbsp butter

Sauce
150 ml/5 fl oz white wine, apple juice or chicken stock (pg 138)
2–3 tbsps Dijon mustard
175 ml/6 fl oz crème fraîche or double cream
Salt and black pepper
Fresh parsley or chives

Eat with:
Green salad (pg 140)
Tomato & onion salad (pg 140)
Watercress

Old School Cornish Pasties

For 4

Shortcrust pastry
225 g/8 oz plain white flour
Good pinch of salt
110 g/4 oz cold butter
2–3 tbsps very cold water
Beaten egg and milk
  for brushing

Filling
225 g/8 oz lean beef steak
  (rump or best stewing)
1 medium onion,
  finely chopped
2 medium potatoes,
  diced small
2 tbsps stock or oil
Pinch dried thyme or
  other herb
1 tbsp parsley,
  finely chopped
Salt and freshly ground
  black pepper

Eat with:
Brown sauce
Ketchup (pg 139)
Mash (pg 22)
Baked beans
Green bean spaghetti (pg 53)

why not?
Eat cold in a picnic
or pack-up.

Traditional potato and meat pasties are true food heroes and surprisingly easy to make. Treat the twisty bit on top as a kind of handle. PS Originally they'd have jam or fruit in one end so the tin miners could get a 2 in 1 meal. Suppose you could try it…

Method
1. Preheat oven to 200°C/400°F/gas 6.
2. **Pastry:** See pg 138 and follow the hand method.
3. **Filling:** Cut any fat off the meat and discard. Cut it into chunks. Then into small pieces.
4. Slap it into a bowl with the onion, potato, stock or oil, herbs and seasoning. Mix together.
5. Divide the pastry into 4. Roll the first piece out into a square on a lightly floured board. Sit a 15 cm/6 in plate in the middle. Cut round it. Repeat with remainder for 4 circles. Roll a bit more if it looks too thick.
6. Heap filling into the centre of each one. Dampen edges of each circle with a bit of water. Pull the opposite sides up and together over the filling. Join them firmly together, pressing between a thumb and finger.
7. Brush with beaten egg and milk. Sit them on a baking tray.
8. Cook for 15–20 minutes then reduce the heat to 190°C/375°F/gas 5 for another 20 minutes. Browning fast? Cover with paper.

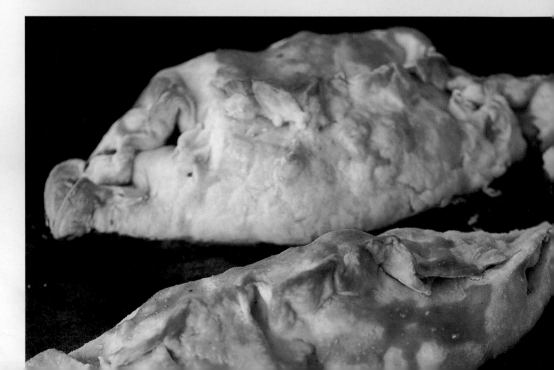

Corned Beef Hash

I love this. It's got style (US style). It's simple – always a good thing. You can chuck it together when you're half asleep so it makes a great all-day breakfast. The ingredients are pretty basic so they're always there waiting. The chilli twist makes it pretty special.

Method

1. Put a pan of lightly salted water on to boil. Add the potato chunks. Boil for 7–10 minutes or till just tender. Don't let them crumble. Drain well.

2. Heat the oil in a heavy based frying pan. Gently fry the onion, garlic and chilli powder for 5 minutes or until softened, not coloured.

3. Add the potatoes. Turn with a spatula and cook gently for a few minutes till hot and coated. Put grill on to heat.

4. Break the corned beef up using two forks so it crumbles into uneven bits. Slap the beef into the mix and turn for a few minutes to heat. Try not to break up the potatoes.

5. Squeeze a good bit of lemon into the hash. Stir in the thyme and season with black pepper and a little salt. Spoon the mix into a shallow ovenproof dish.

6. Sit the dish on a grill pan under a preheated grill for a few minutes till the top catches. Use this time to poach some eggs if you like.

For 3–4
3 medium potatoes, peeled and cut into 1 x 4 cm/ ½ x 1½ in chunks
2 tbsps olive oil
1 large onion, roughly chopped
2 cloves garlic, crushed
Pinch of chilli powder
175 g/6 oz corned beef
Juice of ½ lemon
Few leaves of fresh thyme
Salt and black pepper

Eat with:
Horseradish sauce
Ketchup (pg 139)
Brown sauce
A shake of Tabasco
Baked beans

why not?
Substitute any of:
Cooked ham or bacon
Fried mushrooms
Fried chorizo
Drained tuna
for beef.

Luscious Shepherd's Pie

Get best minced lamb from the butcher, or mince your own. Top it off with the creamiest mash baked to crunchy-topped perfection. Liv loves this. (Ain't made from shepherds.)

Method

1. Heat the olive oil in a large pan or casserole. Cook onion and garlic gently for 5 minutes or till soft, not coloured.
2. Chuck in carrot and celery. Cook to soften for another few minutes.
3. Increase heat and slap in the lamb. Turn with a wooden spoon till browned. Too much fat produced? Spoon it off and chuck it.
4. Add the wine on high heat. Bubble it up to burn off the alcohol.
5. Add stock or water. Chuck in tomato purée, Worcester sauce, lemon juice, chutney, herbs, salt and pepper. Stir. Boil for a few minutes.
6. Reduce heat. Cover the pan. Simmer for 30–60 minutes. Check and stir occasionally. Mix looks dry? Add a splash more liquid.
7. Remove. Add yogurt if using. Taste and adjust seasoning.
8. **Cooking soon?** Cool for a bit then top. **Cooking next day?** Chill ready-topped or skim fat off the cold filling. Top it with mash and cook it for longer.
9. Preheat oven to 200°C/400°F/gas 6.
10. **Topping: Either** boil scrubbed unpeeled potatoes in lightly salted water until tender. Drain. Put them through a ricer before beating in the warm milk, mustard if using, butter and seasoning. **Or** boil peeled and quartered spuds in lightly salted water until tender. Drain. Slap back into the pan to sit on the heat, shaking for a few seconds. Add warm milk, butter, mustard and seasoning. Mash with a masher or fork.
11. Spoon the mash over the meat. Rough up the surface with a fork. Or stick it in a wide-nozzle piping bag and pipe to cover.
12. Bake for 30–40 minutes or till crunchy-topped and brown with bubbling edges.

For 4
1 tbsp olive oil
1 onion, diced
3 cloves garlic, crushed
1 carrot, diced
1 stick celery, diced
450 g/1 lb best minced lamb
4 tbsps red wine
300 ml/10 fl oz chicken stock (pg 138) or water
2 tbsps tomato purée
Dash Worcester sauce
Squeeze of lemon juice
1 tsp mango chutney
Parsley/thyme/oregano/mint/rosemary
1–2 tbsps natural yogurt (optional)
Salt and black pepper

Topping
900 g/2 lbs potatoes
Milk
Mustard (optional)
Butter
Salt and pepper

Eat with:
Carrot pasta (pg 73)
Broccoli (pg 72)
Green bean spaghetti (pg 53)

variations

CHEESY SHEPHERD
At STEP 11 sprinkle with grated Cheddar or Gruyère cheese.
COTTAGE PIE
At STEP 3 add 450 g/1 lb best minced beef instead of lamb.
BEAN FREAKS
At STEP 5 add a small tin of baked beans.

Chic Champ

For 4
900 g/2 lbs old floury
  potatoes, unpeeled and
  scrubbed (King Edwards
  and Maris Pipers work)
3 cloves garlic
200 ml/7 fl oz milk
4 spring onions, finely
  chopped
3 tbsps parsley, finely
  chopped
50–110 g/2–4 oz butter
Salt and black pepper

Eat with:
Grilled bacon
Good baked sausages
Portobello mushrooms

---

variation
COLCANNON
At STEP 7 add 6 tbsps
drained shredded
cooked cabbage.

ALIGOT
At STEP 7 add 2
handfuls grated
Gruyère or Cheddar.

If you've got style and you're a mash fan, then you'll love this creamy Irish classic. A bit like designer food, there's so much taste to it. Not one to eat before going to the gym, I think.

Method
1. Bring a large pan of lightly salted water to boil. Add the whole potatoes and garlic.
2. Boil for 20 minutes or till tender. Test by poking with a knife.
3. While spuds cook, heat the milk in a pan with the spring onions and parsley for 4 minutes. Set aside.
4. Drain spuds. Remove and save garlic. Return spuds to the pan. Shake over the heat for 2 minutes to dry.
5. Remove. Peel carefully while still hot. Protect your hands with a tea towel.
6. Tip spuds back into the cooking pan with two thirds of the butter and peeled garlic. Mash well till smooth with masher or fork.
7. Reheat onion/herb milk till nearly boiled. Use a wooden spoon to beat it into the mash a bit at a time for a creamy, smooth mix. You may not need it all. Taste and season well. Adjust if you need to.
8. Pile champ on a plate. Slap butter in hollow in centre. Lovely.

Patatas Bravas

A plate of these big chunks of lovely spuds with a fiery tomato sauce and cooling garlic mayo (aioli) on the side makes a great Spanish-style way with your potatoes.

Method

1. Sauce: Heat the olive oil in a saucepan. Gently fry the onion till softened but not coloured. Add the garlic, chillies and paprika. Cook for another minute.

2. Add the fresh or canned tomatoes, sugar, salt, optional bay leaf and a few shakes of Tabasco. Bring to the boil then reduce the heat and simmer gently for at least 30 minutes.

3. Patatas: Meantime, heat olive oil in a large pan. Slip raw or parboiled spuds in (parboiled can be fluffier). Cook over a low heat, turning frequently so they brown evenly for at least 20 minutes. Don't rush the frying. Texture matters.

4. Remove spuds from the pan when crisp and golden. Quickly fry the whole chilli if using.

5. Finish sauce: Sieve, then pour it over and around the potatoes. Sprinkle bit of herb over. Sit chilli on top. Slap dollop of aioli on the side. Eat hot or warm. Cool and spicy. Good with griddled chicken or tuna.

For 4

Sauce

2 tbsps olive oil
1 onion, finely chopped
1 clove garlic, crushed
1–2 red chillies, de-seeded and finely chopped
1/2 tsp paprika or smoked paprika
1 x 400 g/14 oz can or 4 large chopped fresh tomatoes
1/2 tsp sugar
Pinch of sea salt
1 bay leaf (optional)
Tabasco sauce

Patatas

3 tbsps olive oil
450 g/1 lb potatoes, peeled and roughly chopped, raw or parboiled for 5 mins
Chilli for topping (optional)
Finely chopped fresh coriander to garnish
Aioli (pg 139)

Eat with:

Tapas (cold meats, hot chorizo, cheeses, prawns, bread, mussels, olives)

Beautiful Blinis & Sexy Salmon

For 4
Salmon
25 g/1 oz Maldon sea salt
25 g/1 oz caster sugar
Finely grated rind of 1 lemon
1 tsp ground black pepper
2 tbsps fresh dill, finely chopped
450 g/1 lb piece salmon fillet

Pancakes
450 g/1 lb potatoes, peeled and quartered
60 g/2½ oz self-raising flour
3 medium eggs, beaten
150 ml/5 fl oz milk
150 ml/5 fl oz double cream
2 extra egg whites
Sunflower oil and butter

Lemon Dressing
3 tbsps caster sugar
50 ml/2 fl oz water
Juice of 2 fat lemons
6 cardamon pods, crushed
150 ml/5 fl oz olive oil

Eat with:
Green leaves with lemon dressing
Sour cream
Horseradish sauce
Dill & mustard mayo (pg 139)

How cool does this look? Curing your own salmon is easy and a perfect excuse to make up these top pancakes. They're so light and fluffy. Everything needs prepping ahead. A sharp-tasting mayo and gorgeous lemon salad dressing makes this dish plate heaven.

Method
1. **Salmon:** Mix salt, sugar, lemon rind, pepper and dill in a bowl.
2. Check salmon for stray bones. Pull out or use tweezers.
3. Lay fish skin-side down on a bit of clingfilm that's big enough to wrap it up in. Spread salt mix evenly over salmon.
4. Wrap completely. Sit fish on large dish or tray. Slap a chopping board on top and then weights or tins to compress it.
5. Leave in the fridge for 2–3 days to cure. It will seep. Doesn't matter. Ready to eat? Wipe off the cure. Slice thinly with a sharp knife.
6. **Lemon dressing:** Tip sugar, water, lemon juice, cardamon pods in a small pan. Boil. Reduce heat to low. Simmer for 5 mins. Leave to cool.
7. Whisk in olive oil and season.
8. **Pancakes:** Boil spuds for 10–15 minutes or till soft (poke with a knife). Drain. Mash with a masher or fork till really smooth. Cover when cold and fridge it.
9. Later on or the next day let mash return to room temperature. Sift the flour into it. Add the eggs a bit at a time using a wooden spoon and/or balloon whisk to make a thick smooth batter. May need effort!
10. Heat milk and cream in a small pan till hot (don't boil). Beat or whisk very slowly into the batter.
11. Whisk the extra whites till soft and huge. Fold into batter with a metal spoon. Don't fuss about the odd bit of white.
12. Heat a bit of oil and butter in a large pan. When hot, drop large tablespoons of mix to cook for 1–2 minutes each side till browning and cooked through.
13. Cover and keep warm till all done.
14. Plate salmon, blinis and mayo. Toss leaves in lemon dressing. Serve the queue. Delicious.

Chocolate

I love a bit of chocolate. Hey it got me into my big passion – cooking. The smell of the lovely stuff melting down ready for use in whatever you like. Licking out the bowl when Mum'd made chocolate cake. So I stole this chapter for myself and I'm here to share an awesome ingredient. Rules first: chocolate can be difficult (bit like this cat) so treat it with respect. If you're melting it down – do it in a bowl over a pan of lightly simmering water. Don't get water in the bowl or let the base touch the stuff in the pan. It'll seize up and be impossible to deal with. Use best quality chocolate (70% solids) for top results. Don't keep choc-coated stuff in the fridge. Chilling whacks the sheen off it. Chocolate's a great mood food. It sweetens you up. But – don't eat too much. Exercise your cooking skills on my brilliant fruit sundaes. Excellent truffle bars. Top birthday cake. Choc fudge pudding. Posh profiteroles. Cocoa's good (very good). Slap it into meringues for a dusky crunch. Get it into crêpes. Short on time? Melt it down to pour over ice-cream. Coat fresh fruit like my wacky banana sticks. Get creative. I sculpted my face in it for Art GCSE – then ate it. I've never had a mate who doesn't love chocolate.

Top Chocolate Soufflé

For 4
3 large egg yolks
4 large egg whites
50 g/2 oz good dark
  chocolate
150 ml/¼ pint milk
50 g/2 oz caster sugar
6 drops vanilla extract
1 tbsp cornflour
2 tbsps double cream
Melted butter for greasing
Icing sugar for dusting

This one's a high class bit of chocolate cooking. It's perfect for a posh dinner or to impress someone or both. Soufflé's got a reputation for being tricky but this one ain't that hard. It's light and chocolatey – pretty damn special.

Method

1. Preheat oven to 170°C/325°F/gas 3. Slap a flat baking tray in there.
2. Lightly grease a 15 cm/6 in soufflé dish with melted butter using a pastry brush and upward strokes.
3. Separate eggs into two bowls (with grease-free hands).
4. Break the chocolate up into a small pan with half the milk.

5. Heat extremely gently stirring a bit with a wooden spoon until smooth. Remove.
6. Mix egg yolks, sugar and vanilla in a large bowl. Beat with a whisk till light and moussey.
7. Stir remaining milk and cornflour together till smooth.
8. Add to the egg mix with the melted chocolate. Stir till smooth.
9. Tip sauce into a heavy based pan over a gentle heat. Stir constantly and patiently to keep it smooth as it thickens. Remove as it just starts to bubble.
10. Stir in the cream. Return to a low heat, stirring for 2 minutes. Scrape mix into a large bowl.
11. Whisk egg whites till stiff and voluminous. Tip into chocolate mix. Fold in with a large metal spoon and big scooping movements.
12. Pour into soufflé dish. Cook on baking tray for 30 minutes till risen, firm on top but a bit wobbly. If top browns up early cover with greaseproof. (Shut oven door slowly or it sinks.) Dust with icing sugar. Scoff immediately.

For 4–6
Butterscotch sauce
25 g/1 oz butter
2 tbsps golden syrup
175 g/6 oz soft brown sugar
4 tbsps single cream
Crêpes
75 g /3 oz plain white flour
25 g/1 oz cocoa
1 egg
225 ml/8 fl oz milk
A splash of water
Butter for frying
Icing sugar
Filling
Vanilla ice-cream, try
  homemade (pg 117)
Morello cherry jam, fresh
  de-stoned cherries or
  poached cherries
Lime juice

Choc Cherry Crêpes

Another variation on the classic pancake. This one is gorgeous. A top contender for Valentine's Day. It's pretty rich so don't overdo it. Get ice-cream out of the freezer before you get cooking.

Method

1. Butterscotch sauce: Melt butter, syrup and sugar together in a small pan. Boil. Stir in cream. Reheat gently. Remove.

2. Crêpes: Sift flour and cocoa into large bowl. Make a dent and crack the egg and a bit of milk in. Using a balloon whisk or wooden spoon beat together, adding milk and water gradually for a smooth batter.

3. Put crêpe pan or frying pan on a high heat. Brush with butter or drop a bit in to melt. Tip to coat the base so your crêpe won't stick when you cook it. (If it does – just chuck it!)

4. Pour 2–3 tablespoons batter into the pan with a swirling motion, twisting to coat. Cook for 1–2 minutes.

5. Toss the crêpe to cook other side or turn neatly with a spatula.

6. Fill: Lay on plate. Spoon ice-cream, a bit of warm jam, cherries and a squeeze of lime onto a quarter. Fold. Fold again. Drizzle with butterscotch sauce and lime. Dust with icing sugar.

variations

Try one of these filllings:
CHESTNUT LIME
MAPLE SYRUP
Chopped marron
glacé, vanilla ice, maple
syrup, lime
BANANA
BUTTERSCOTCH
Sliced banana, vanilla
ice, butterscotch
sauce, lemon
PEACH RASPBERRY
Sliced peach or
nectarine, vanilla ice,
fresh raspberry sauce
MANGO LIME
COCONUT
Sliced mango, coconut
ice, maple syrup, lime

Chocolate Nut Brownies

Makes 16
50 g/2 oz dark chocolate
110 g/4 oz soft butter
225 g/8 oz light soft brown
  sugar
2 eggs, beaten
50 g/2 oz plain flour
Pinch of salt
1/2 tsp baking powder
225 g/8 oz walnuts/pecans
6 drops vanilla extract
Grated rind 1/2 large orange

Don't panic. They'll crack up in the tin. But it's a cool look and these chewy brownies taste fantastic. Make a batch at the weekend to snack on through the week. Take them into school to share with mates. Throw some raisins in for a fruity twist. Don't like nuts? Go for my truffle bars.

Method
1. Preheat oven to 190°C/375°F/gas 5.
2. Grease and line the bottom of a 20 cm/8 in square shallow loose-based baking tin.
3. Put a pan of water on to heat until it simmers.
4. Break chocolate into a heatproof bowl. Sit the bowl on the pan. Check that the base sits clear of the gently simmering water.
5. When the chocolate melts stir till smooth with a wooden spoon. Take it off the heat and the pan.
6. Tip the butter and sugar into a large bowl. Beat hard with a wooden spoon till it's soft and creamy.
7. Dribble the beaten eggs into the butter mix gradually, beating furiously as you go. Stir in the melted chocolate, flour, salt, baking powder, nuts, vanilla and orange rind. Transfer to the tin and level gently.
8. Bake for 35–40 minutes. Test with a toothpick. It should come out clean. Leave in the tin for 15 minutes.
9. Divide into 16 squares with a sharp knife. Remove with a spatula. Sit on a cooling rack.

Excellent Chocolate Truffle Bars

Like brownies but better I think. These are nut-free, smooth and deeply chocolatey. They're perfect with a cup of tea or at the end of a meal with a pot of coffee. Why not decorate them to look like posh chocolates? Sure to be a hit whatever.

Method

1. Preheat oven to 180°C/350°F/gas 4. Line a 20 cm/8 in square baking tin with baking paper.

2. Break the chocolate up. Tip it and the butter into a heatproof bowl.

3. Sit it over a pan of gently simmering water checking that the base does not touch the water. Let the two melt and then stir them together.

4. Take the bowl off the heat. Beat in the sugar and vanilla.

5. Use a balloon whisk to beat in the eggs. Sift in the flour and salt. Give the mix a good beating.

6. Tip the truffle into the tin. Cook for 35 minutes. Check for doneness with a cocktail stick. You want it still a bit moist.

7. Remove from the oven to cool on a rack. Mark up into bars after 10 minutes. Use a spatula to remove from the tin when cold.

Makes 8 bars
200 g/7 oz dark chocolate
150 g/5 oz butter
225 g/8 oz caster sugar
2 tsps vanilla extract
2 large eggs
1 extra yolk
75 g/3 oz plain flour
Pinch of salt

Optional icing
Stir a few drops of water into 6 tbsps sifted icing sugar for a stiffish mix. Pipe decorations.

Frozen Chocolate Banana Sticks

Makes 8–12
4 bananas
8–12 ice-lolly sticks or
   wooden skewers
275 g/10 oz good chocolate
   (milk or plain)

variations
CRISPY
Mix rice crispies into
part or all of the
chocolate.
COCONUT
Sprinkle desiccated
coconut over the
chocolate.

why not?
Make apple sticks.
Dip apples on sticks
into melted chocolate.
Sit upside down on
greaseproof to dry.

Dip fruit on stalks
(cherries,
strawberries, Chinese
gooseberries).

Bake choc bananas.
Preheat oven to
200°C/400°F/gas 6.
Make a slit down
unpeeled bananas. Slip
some chocolate
buttons or a bit of
bubbly chocolate in.
Wrap in foil. Cook for
10–15 minutes.

Now these look a bit weird. They could almost pass for pieces of art. Think banana split without the ice-cream. They make a tasty laugh at the end of a meal or make up a load to cool down a party.

Method
1. Lay a sheet of non-stick paper on a baking tray.
2. Peel the bananas.
3. **Either:** Cut each in half. Shove an ice-lolly stick or skewer into each cut end to make a lollipop.
Or: Cut each into 4 diagonal slices. Stick a skewer into each one.
4. Lay the lollies on the paper. Slap into the freezer for an hour or till well frozen.
5. Put a small pan of water on to simmer gently. Sit a bowl over the top checking it's clear of the water.
6. Break up the chocolate. Slap into the bowl. Once it melts stir to a smooth sauce.
7. Fetch bananas. Dunk in chocolate to coat or use a spoon.
8. Prop in a glass or stick in a grapefruit while setting.
9. Lay back on the tray. Freeze. Store in freezer bags or boxes.

Sleepover Breakfast Brioche

There's nothing like tearing into one of these in the morning. But be warned. I've burnt myself on the oozy chocolate inside many a time. Let it cool for a second or two before you dig in. These look, smell and taste so good you can't help thinking they should be on an advert.

Makes 12

275 g/10 oz strong white
  bread flour
1 x 7 g sachet easy blend
  dried yeast
Pinch of fine salt
3 medium eggs, beaten
40 g/1½ oz caster sugar
55 ml/2 fl oz warm milk
110 g/4 oz soft butter
12 squares from a bar of
  plain chocolate or a good
  Belgian chocolate spread
Extra beaten egg for
  brushing

Method

1. By mixer: Tip flour, yeast, salt, eggs, sugar and milk into mixer bowl with dough hook. Beat for 5 minutes. **By hand:** Sift flour and salt into a large bowl, adding sugar and yeast. Tip eggs and milk into a dent in the centre. Beat to a smooth dough with hands or a wooden spoon. Sit dough on a floured board. Knead, punch, slap, stretch for 5 minutes for a smooth, elastic ball.

2. Both: Now, smear a bit of butter onto the dough. Push, punch and squeeze it right in till amalgamated. Repeat till all butter's used, the dough shiny and bubbly.

3. Put dough into a large bowl. Cover with clingfilm. Chill in fridge for at least 1 hour or overnight if cooking for breakfast.

4. Grease individual brioche tins. Sit on baking tray. Or grease muffin or bun tins.

5. Knead dough. Divide and make into 12 smooth flat circles. Sit a choc square or half a teaspoon choc spread in the centre. Draw the dough up round it. Join with firm pressure and a bit of beaten egg for a smooth ball and no leakage.

6. Drop into tins join side down. Leave in a warm place to double in size. Preheat oven to 200°C/400°F/gas 6.

7. Brush with beaten egg. Bake 12–15 minutes till browned and high. Cool on a rack for 3 minutes or eat cold.

variation

OTHER FILLINGS
Apricot or strawberry jam
Choc hazelnut spread
Try them plain

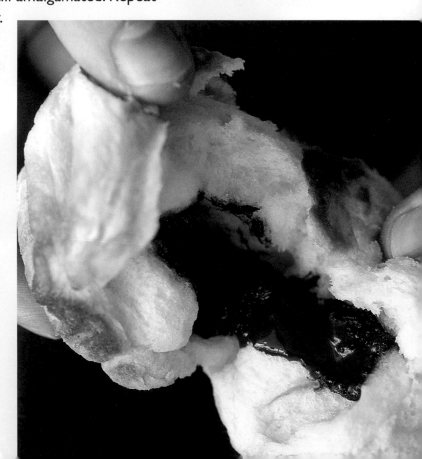

Hot Chocolate Fudge Pudding

For 4
1 tsp instant coffee
1½ tbsp boiling water
110 g/4 oz soft butter
110 g/4 oz caster sugar
2 medium eggs
½–1 tsp vanilla bean paste
  or vanilla extract
110 g/4 oz self-raising flour
25 g/1 oz cocoa
Icing sugar for topping

Sauce
1 level tbsp cocoa powder
110 g/4 oz soft brown
  sugar
150 ml/¼ pint hot water

Eat with: Vanilla ice-cream
(pg 117).

You've got to take this one on trust. When you get it in the dish it looks like a cruel joke. Get it out of the oven though and you've got this delicious chocolate sponge over a delectable sauce. Slap this together for parents – you'll never get grounded…

Method

1. Preheat oven to 180°C/350°F/gas 4.
2. Grease base and sides of a 850 ml/1½ pint ovenproof dish.
3. Mix coffee and boiling water, stirring to dissolve.
4. Slap butter and sugar into a large bowl. Beat with a wooden spoon till well light, pale, creamy.
5. Beat eggs with a fork. Add to the mix bit by bit, beating as you go. Add a pinch of flour if it threatens to curdle. When creamy, add vanilla. Sift the flour and cocoa in. Add the liquid coffee.
6. Fold everything together using a large metal spoon and light scooping movements till it just falls off the end of your spoon.
7. Spoon into the dish, levelling the top.
8. Sauce: Mix the brown sugar and cocoa in a bowl. Stir in the hot water. Pour over the sponge. Looks crazy. Stay with it!
9. Sit it in a roasting tin with enough boiling water to reach half way up the sides. Cook for 45 minutes or longer till well risen. A toothpick should come out clean. Sift icing sugar. Eat hot, warm or cold. Scrummy…

Chocolate Fruit Sundaes

An awesome American hero. Make it simple or extravagant. Chuck loads of fruit in there. Not just for Sundaes.

Method

1. Ice-cream: Tip eggs into a bowl. Beat well with a fork.

2. Pour milk into a pan. Add sugar and vanilla paste or seeds scraped from a pod. Heat gently, stirring with a wooden spoon to dissolve sugar. Whack the heat up. Bring milk just to boiling point (bubbling). Remove.

3. Tip it into the egg, stirring continuously. Tip back into pan.

4. Heat gently, stirring till the custard thickens enough to coat the back of the spoon. (If it curdles at any stage, remove and beat till smooth.)

5. Cool custard then beat yogurt in with balloon whisk. Churn in ice-cream maker or pour cream into a bowl or freezer bag. Freeze till it starts to solidify. Remove and re-whisk. Return to freezer. Remove 10 minutes before you need it.

6. Fruit: Wash and prepare your chosen fruit.

7. Chocolate sauce: Break the chocolate into a heatproof bowl. Place over a pan of gently simmering water. Add butter, syrup and water. Melt then stir till smooth. Remove from heat. Add the vanilla extract.

8. Enjoy yourself: Chuck alternate layers of ice-cream, fruit, optional meringue and chocolate sauce into sundae or other glasses.

For 4
Good bought vanilla ice-cream or your own:
6 egg yolks
150 ml/¼ pint milk
60 g /2½ oz caster sugar
Seeds of 1 vanilla pod, or
   ½–1 tsp vanilla bean paste
250 ml/9 fl oz plain yogurt

My chocolate sauce
110 g/4 oz plain chocolate
10 g/½ oz butter
2 tbsps golden syrup
2 tbsps water
1 tbsp natural vanilla extract

Choice of fresh fruit
Stone, chop or peel…
Cherries
Raspberries
Strawberries
Pear
Bananas
Chinese gooseberries
Blackberries

Meringue
3–4 plain or chocolate meringues (pg 121), crumbled

why not?

Make Knickerbocker Glory. Stack loads more fresh fruit layered with chopped jelly (pg 126), fresh raspberry sauce (pg 133) and crumbled amaretti biscuits.

Best Chocolate Cake

For 10
50 g/2 oz plain flour
60 g/2½ oz ground almonds
225 g/8 oz good quality dark chocolate (at least 70% cocoa solids)
225 g/8 oz butter
6 eggs, separated
50 g/2 oz soft brown sugar
Little grated orange rind (optional)
175 g/6 oz caster sugar
Icing sugar

Makes a damn fine teatime or birthday style treat. The dip in the middle's deliberate. Love it.

Method
1. Preheat oven to 180°C/350°F/gas 4.
2. Grease and line base and sides of a 20 cm/8 in loose base or clip sided tin with greaseproof paper.
3. Sift flour and almonds into a big bowl.
4. Put chocolate squares and butter into a heatproof bowl. Sit over a pan of gently simmering water with the base clear. Melt. Stir till smooth. Remove. Cool a bit.
5. Separate eggs into 2 large bowls.
6. Whisk brown sugar and egg yolks together for a few minutes to get a pale frothy mousse. Add the flour mix, chocolate and rind if using. Fold lightly to mix using a large metal spoon and scooping movements.
7. Whisk the egg whites till soft and well frothy. Add caster sugar gradually for a stiff meringue. Fold gently into the cake mix. Tip into tin. Bake for 45–50 minutes till crisp on top, squidgy inside. Test with a cocktail stick – should exit a bit sticky.
8. Cool on rack. The cake will sink but that's OK. Peel paper off with care when cold. Dust with icing sugar.

Posh Choc Profiteroles

Retro French classic. Crisp pastry puffs meet soft vanilla cream and rich chocolate drizzle. Stack 'em up for posh puddings, teatimes, dinner parties, parties. Gorgeous.

Method

1. Puffs: Cover a large plate with a piece of greaseproof paper. Sift the flour, salt and sugar onto it.

2. Tip the water and butter into a medium sized pan. Melt gently. Increase the heat to bring to the boil. Immediately slide the dry ingredients off the paper into the boiling liquid in one go. Beat like mad with a wooden spoon till the dough makes a ball. Whip off the heat. Beat furiously for a few minutes to make a smooth paste. Slap the greaseproof back on the plate. Tip the paste onto it. Leave for at least 10 minutes.

3. Preheat oven to 200°C/400°F/gas 6. Grease two large baking trays.

4. Slap the paste into a bowl. Beat the egg in a little at a time. The final mix wants to be soft and glossy and should just drop off your spoon. You may not need all the egg or you may need more of it.

5. Heap teaspoons of mix well apart on baking trays. Gently flatten any spikes with your fingers. Sprinkle a few drops of cold water on the trays between puffs to aid rising.

6. Cook for 20–25 mins or till well browned and crisp. Remove. Pierce base of each with a skewer. Cook for 5 mins upside down to crisp. Cool on rack.

7. Fill: Whisk cream till just stiff. Fold in sugar and vanilla. Spoon into piping bag with large nozzle. Pipe through holes to fill puffs or split and fill.

8. Make choc sauce. Sit puffs on plates or bowls. Drizzle 'em.

Makes 20–25
Puffs
100 g/3½ oz strong white flour
Pinch of salt
Pinch of caster sugar
200 ml/7 fl oz water
75 g/3 oz butter
2 large eggs, beaten
Filling
570 ml/1 pint double cream or whipping cream
1–2 tbsps icing sugar, sifted
A few drops vanilla extract
Sauce
Hot chocolate sauce (pg 117)

variations

COFFEE ÉCLAIRS
At STEP 5 pipe éclair style lengths of paste well apart on the baking sheets. At STEP 7 pipe cream into each éclair. At STEP 8 make up a batch of coffee icing: Beat 225g/8 oz sifted icing sugar with 2 tbsps of very strong, hot coffee with a wooden spoon till soft and just runny. Dip the top of each éclair into the icing. Let it set.

ICE-CREAM BUNS
Make ice-cream buns. Fill larger puffs with ice-cream (pg 117). Drizzle chocolate sauce. Eat at once.

Chocolate Orange Cookies

Makes 16

150 g/5 oz soft butter
175 g/6 oz caster sugar
225 g/8 oz plain white flour
2 tsps baking powder
1 pinch ground cinnamon
75 g/3 oz dark or milk
  chocolate
Grated rind of 1 orange
1½ tbsps orange juice

As the classic cookie always does, this one goes well with a glass of milk. So what are you waiting for? Get down and make 'em… Delicious.

Method

1. Preheat oven to 180°C/350°F/gas 4. Grease 2 large baking trays with extra butter.
2. Tip the butter and sugar into a large bowl. Beat furiously with a wooden spoon till mixed, pale and creamy.
3. Sift the flour, baking powder and cinnamon directly into the bowl.
4. Chop the chocolate into smallish bits with a sharp knife on a flat wooden board. Tip it into the bowl. Add orange rind and juice.
5. Use a fork to mix everything to a stiff paste. Pull it together firmly with your fingers. The heat binds the dough. Roll it into a ball.

6. Sit the dough on a lightly floured board. Use a floured rolling pin to roll it out to 1 cm/½ in thickness. Cut into rounds with a 6 cm/2½ in cutter. It will be bumpy. No problem.
7. Sit the biscuits well apart on the baking trays. They spread. Bake for 20–25 minutes or until pale gold colour. Remove.
8. Sprinkle with a little caster sugar. Leave on trays for 5 minutes. Transfer to a wire rack to crisp up and cool. Store in an airtight container.

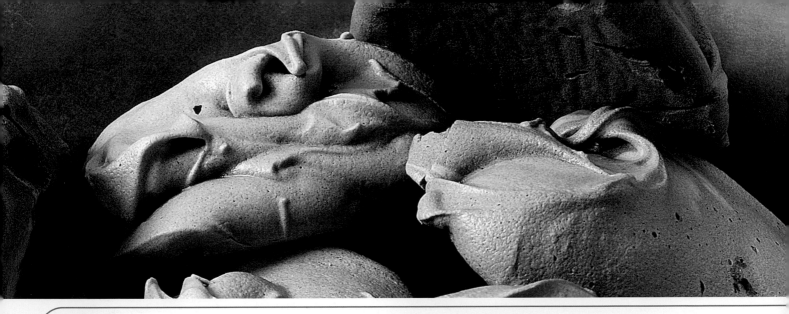

Cocoa Crunch Meringues

I love meringues but these chocolatey ones just blow me away. Stack them on a plate with some plain white ones for stunning looks and dramatic contrast.

Method
1. Preheat oven to 130°C/250°F/gas ½.
2. Line 2 large baking trays with greaseproof paper.
3. Stick your egg whites in a greasefree bowl – I use a copper one. Whisk with an electric or hand whisk till you get soft white peaks. Add the sugar a bit at a time, whisking as you go till the meringue is really stiff and white.
4. Sift the cocoa powder over the mix. Fold it in using a large metal spoon and big scooping movements – the odd whitish streak is fine.
5. Get the mix onto the trays using two large spoons. Make a lot of small meringues or a few big ones. Use one spoon to push the mix off the other. Leave a bit of space between meringues to allow spreading. If

you want to get fancy use a piping bag with medium–large nozzle.
6. Stick the trays into your oven. Bake for 1½ hours. Turn off the heat.
7. Leave the meringues there till quite cold. Peel them carefully off the paper. Store in an airtight container for up to 2 months.

Makes 8
4 egg whites
225 g/8 oz caster sugar
1 tbsp cocoa powder

Eat with: Macerated strawberries (slice large berries; sprinkle with a bit of icing sugar and lemon juice; chill till needed), sliced peaches, mangoes marinated in lime syrup (pg 137).

variation
PAVLOVA
Spread the mix into two flat circles on the baking trays. Cook for the same time as individual meringues. When cold, sandwich with whipped cream and fresh berries.

Sweet Stuff

Everyone loves a pudding and Vez is no exception. We're talking elite eating here. Quality cooking. OK there's sugar playing in most of these beautiful dishes but no problem. Just don't scoff the lot yourself while chained to the sofa. Balance a slice of something good with a game or two. Making this beautiful stuff's like a culinary workout anyway. You get to perfect key toning techniques like whisking, beating, grating, folding in, creaming. Puds are also a great excuse to eat fruit. Baked apples with dates (meringue-topped or not). Cinnamon toast with summer plums. Whole orange cake (yup you use the whole fruit). Sherbet lemon jelly. Summer pudding. Raspberry ripple fool. Styley ice-creams majoring on fruitiness. All these dishes are perfect for serving when you've got mates over. Special dinners. Birthdays. Weekends when you're relaxing. Treating a parent who's been behaving. (Or maybe you need a favour.) Game set and match – this stuff's the fittest.

American Pancakes

For 4
2 medium–large eggs at
    room temperature
150 ml/¹/₄ pint milk
50 g/2 oz melted butter
110 g/4 oz plain flour
10 g/¹/₂ oz caster sugar
2 pinches salt
2 tsps baking powder
Extra melted butter for
    brushing

Cooking for breakfast?
Great with maple syrup,
blackberries, any berries
and crisply grilled bacon.

Eating for lunch?
Try with chopped smoked
salmon and sour cream.

Teatime?
Good with jam (pg 138),
cream and strawberries, or
just butter.

I fell in love with these in America. They're light and
fluffy with a golden finish and are easily adapted for any
eating situation. OK they take a minute more to make
than crêpes but so what? Stack and style any way you
want. Sweet or savoury we're talking quality.

Method

1. Separate eggs. Slap yolks and whites into different bowls.

2. Beat yolks well with a fork. Add milk and melted butter till blended.

3. Sift flour, sugar, salt and baking powder into a large third bowl. Add
the egg/milk mix to it. Stir in gradually and gently for a lump-free batter.

4. Whisk the egg whites until they are stiff and white but still soft, not
overbeaten.

5. Tip into the batter then fold in as gently as you can using a large
metal spoon and soft scooping movements.

6. Heat a heavy bottomed frying pan. Coat with a bit of melted butter
(pastry brush works). Drop tablespoons of the mix in when hot enough.

7. Cook 1–2 minutes per side. Should be golden on the outside with
puffed up middles.

8. Eat now or keep warm.

Sweet US Shortcakes

Like scones but double-stacked with a sweeter crumbly texture. Butter and jam them up or get some cream and fresh fruit in there. Perfect with a cup of tea – preferably from a proper teapot.

Method

1. Preheat oven to 230°C/450°F/gas 8.
2. Sift flour, baking powder and salt into a large bowl.
3. Chuck the butter in, cutting into small bits. Get it into the flour by rubbing the two between your fingertips, hand held over the bowl, till the mix looks like breadcrumbs.
4. Slap in sugar and cream. Mix with a fork. Pull mix into a soft ball with your fingers. Handle lightly now.
5. Sit dough on a lightly floured board. Shape and smooth lightly before gently rolling out till 1 cm/½ in thickness.
6. Cut into 5 cm/ 2 in rounds with a plain cutter. Don't twist it.
7. Reform remaining dough gently. Re-roll and cut again.
8. Sit half the cakes well apart on a greased baking tray.
9. Brush lightly with melted butter. Sit a plain circle firmly on top to double stack.
10. Bake for 10–15 minutes till golden and cooked through. Cool on a rack.

For 6
275 g/10 oz plain flour
3 tsps baking powder
Pinch of salt
150 g/5 oz soft butter
50 g/2 oz caster sugar
150 ml/¼ pint whipping
   cream
25 g/1 oz melted butter

Sherbet Lemon Jelly

For 4
2 large lemons
110 g/4 oz caster sugar
570 ml/1 pint water
5 leaves of gelatine

why not?
Make:
FLAT JELLY
Don't whisk it.
ST CLEMENTS
Use the juice of
1 lemon and 1 small
orange.
ORANGE
Use the juice of
2 oranges or blood
oranges, or
4 clementines.
VEGETARIAN?
Sub gelatine with
agar-agar.
FEELING ILL?
Ask someone to
make it.

You'll impress your mates with this one. Homemade jelly's so much tastier and healthier than the rubbish packet stuff. This one's got the sharpest taste and neatest look to it. Get yourself some interesting jelly moulds to pour it into.

Method

1. Pare rind thinly from lemons with a sharp knife or peeler. Rough strips are fine. Avoid the bitter white pith.

2. Slap rind, sugar and water into a pan. Bring to the boil for 1 minute. Reduce heat. Simmer very gently with the lid on for 15 minutes. Remove. Tip into bowl. Cool.

3. Squeeze the lemon juice into cold syrup through sieve.

4. Drop gelatine leaves into a bowl of cold water. Remove after 5 minutes. Squeeze moisture out of them.

5. Put them into a small pan over a very low heat to melt. Soon as it happens remove from the heat.

6. Pour the lemon syrup into the melted gelatine immediately (never pour gelatine into the syrup).

7. Refrigerate. When it looks like setting, whisk it hard to create white bubbles.

8. Pour into glasses or splash a jelly mould or glass dish with a bit of water. Pour jelly in. Refrigerate. When it's set get your spoon in there.

Whole Orange Cake

Don't panic. This wacky mix transforms itself into the lightest, loveliest citrusy cake. Make it for afternoon tea or an awesome pudding. Gluten allergy? Get in there.

Method

1. Stick oranges in a medium pan. Cover with water.
2. Boil then reduce heat. Simmer for 2–3 hours with lid on. Top up water when needed. Remove fruit. Leave to cool.
3. Slice fruit in two. Get pips out and chuck them.
4. Stick whole fruit in a processor or blender. Blitz till smooth.
5. Preheat oven to 180°C/350°F/gas 4.
6. Grease and line base and sides of a 23 cm/9 in clip sided tin.
7. Crack eggs into a large bowl with sugar. Whisk to a pale thick mousse which doubles in volume using an electric or hand whisk. It should leave a trail on the surface.
8. Tip the orange blitz, baking powder and almonds into the mousse. Fold together with a large metal spoon using a few big scooping movements. Handle gently to keep the air in.
9. Pour into tin. Bake for 50–60 minutes. Insert a cocktail stick to test it's done. It should come out clean. Cool in the tin.
10. Release tin. Peel paper away. Sift icing sugar over.

For 4–6
2 large unwaxed oranges
6 medium eggs
225 g/8 oz caster sugar
1 tsp baking powder
225 g/8 oz ground almonds
Fresh raspberries (optional)
Icing sugar (optional)

Eat with:
Citrus cream – mix mascarpone, icing sugar, lemon rind, orange and lemon juice into a smooth cream.

variations
OTHER ORANGE OPTIONS
Try subbing 2 large blood oranges or 4–6 clementines for normal oranges.

Classic Crème Caramel

For 4
Butter
2 tbsps cold water
50 g/2 oz granulated sugar
2 tsps boiling water
3 large eggs
275 ml/½ pint milk
25 g/1 oz caster sugar
½ tsp vanilla extract

Enjoy the light silky texture of the baked custard sitting in its soft golden caramel sauce. This classic pudding's comfort food chic. Make it to cheer yourself up. Tart it up with fruit and cream for something special...

Method

1. Preheat oven to 170°C/325°F/gas 3.
2. Grease a 570 ml/1 pint dish with butter.
3. Tip cold water and granulated sugar into a small pan over a low heat. Stir to dissolve with a wooden spoon. Increase heat. Stop stirring to allow syrup to caramelize. Boil till it goes a deep golden brown. Don't let it burn.
4. Carefully remove pan from heat and add boiling water. Pour liquid into buttered dish, tilting it to swirl toffee over the base and a bit up the sides. Set aside.
5. Beat eggs and milk together with a balloon whisk, adding caster sugar and vanilla. Sit a sieve over the caramelized baking dish. Pour the egg mix through it.

6. Stand dish in a roasting tin. Pour cold water into the tin to reach halfway up the sides of the dish.
7. Cook for 45–50 mins till just set. It keeps cooking so you want a bit of wobble.
8. Take it out of tin to cool. Chill.
9. To turn out: Sit a plate over the dish. Invert. Give it a shake. If it doesn't loosen, turn back. Run a thin knife around custard with care. Try again.

Baked Apple Meringues

Mix and match these bad boys. Some with meringue on top. Some not. Either way they're deliciously juicy and full of awesomeness. A really great pud to cheer up autumn days going into winter.

Method

1. Preheat oven to 180°C/350°F/gas 4. Grease an ovenproof dish large enough for all the apples (use double ingredients for big family dinners).

2. Use a sharp knife to cut a continuous line around the circumference of each fruit to stop them bursting. Sit them in the dish.

3. Tip the chopped dates into a small bowl. Mix with the orange rind and juice. Stuff the mix into the centre of the cored fruit.

4. Mix the brown sugar and spice. Sprinkle this mix on top of each apple then dot the lot with dabs of butter.

5. Pour the juice, wine or sherry into the dish. Bake till nearly cooked through. This could take 45 minutes, or much longer if using larger apples or a harder variety. Keep looking, keep checking.

6. Make meringue. Whisk 2 egg whites till soft, white and peaky. Whisk half the sugar in, bit by bit, till mix is very stiff. Stir in the rest.

7. Remove fruit from the oven. Using a spoon and sharp knife peel the top bit of skin off 2 apples. Spoon or pipe meringue on these stripped tops. Return to oven. For soft meringue, bake for 15 minutes. Crisper tops will take longer, but watch the apples don't collapse.

8. Eat hot or warm, and great cold with yogurt or custard. Try reheating.

Makes 4

4 cooking apples (Bramleys work), washed and cored

A few fresh or dried dates, chopped

Grated rind and juice of 1 large orange

150 ml/¼ pint orange juice, apple juice, ginger wine or sherry

2 tbsps soft brown sugar

1 tsp mixed spice

Butter for topping

Meringue

2 egg whites

110 g/4 oz caster sugar

variations

Fill the apple cavities with a mix of golden syrup and butter, or butter, sherry and crumbled amaretti.

Jam Soufflé Omelette

For 1
Filling
1–2 tbsps best jam (pg 138)
A little water

Omelette
2 large fresh eggs (organic
  if possible)
1 tsp caster sugar
1 tbsp milk
A little butter
Icing sugar

Seems a little crazy but you'll be glad you've made it. It's heavy on the WOW factor (both looks and taste) and light in the mouth. Sweet puffy omelette meets hot jammy sauce. I use a 6 inch pan for this. Make your own jam, or buy a best fruity one.

Method

1. Preheat grill to medium.

2. Filling: Tip the jam and water into a small pan to melt. Heat gently, stirring with a wooden spoon until sticky and just runny. Put aside until you need it.

3. Omelette: Separate the eggs. Slap the yolks into one bowl. Whites into another. Put sugar and milk in with the yolks. Using a balloon whisk, beat them into a moussy froth (may take time). Wash the whisk to get it grease-free.

4. Whisk the egg whites so they stand in soft peaks. Don't overwhisk.

5. Put the pan onto a gentle heat with a little butter.

6. Tip whisked whites into the yolk mix. Use a spatula to cut or fold them till just mixed. Keeping air in is vital so odd blobs don't matter.

7. When the butter foams, slide the mix in. Cook for 1–2 minutes or till just set.

8. Slide the pan under the grill but not too close to the heat for 2 minutes. It should rise. Remove when just set and just colouring.

9. Slide onto a warm plate (use spatula to help). Pour jam over half. Use a spatula to fold the other half over. Sift over a little icing sugar. Mmm… Magnificent enough for a special dinner.

Cinnamon Toast with Summer Plums

Mmm … the bread toasts up to a lovely crisp top while the base soaks up the luscious juices from the plums. It's all set off with a buttery cinnamon sweetness. Honestly, you've got to try this.

For 4
75 g/3 oz soft butter
1 tsp ground cinnamon
4 large slices of good white bread, crustless
8 or 10 large ripe plums (600–700 g/1¼–1½ lbs), cut in half and stoned
110 g/4 oz soft brown sugar (or demerara for extra crunch), and extra for topping
Caster sugar (optional)

Method

1. Preheat oven to 190°C/375°F/gas 5.
2. Cream butter and cinnamon in a small bowl.
3. Spread two-thirds evenly over the bread.
4. Sit bread in the base of a well buttered shallow heatproof dish. It may creep up the sides but that doesn't matter.
5. Fill each plum centre with brown sugar. Place cut side down evenly over the bread. Dot remaining butter cinnamon–mix over the top with extra brown sugar.
6. Cover with a bit of buttered baking paper and bake for 20 minutes.
7. Uncover and cook for 5 minutes or till the bread is crisp and browned.
8. Remove. Sprinkle with a bit of caster sugar if you like. Custard?

Summer Pudding

For 6
110 g/4 oz caster sugar
150 ml/¼ pint orange juice
2 tbsps lemon juice
1 tbsp Crème de Cassis
900 g/2 lb mixed soft fruit
(e.g. rhubarb, strawberries,
blackcurrants, redcurrants,
raspberries)
2–3 mint leaves (optional)
6–8 thin slices of white
bread
Fruit for decorating
(optional)
Cream for piping (optional)

Don't be put off by the bread. It soaks up those oozy fruity juices and transforms itself into something extraordinary. PS Cheat in winter. Buy frozen summer fruit.

Method
1. Tip sugar, fruit juices and Crème de Cassis into a large pan on gentle heat to dissolve sugar. Bring to the boil then decrease heat.
2. Add rhubarb if using (cook 3 minutes) then strawberries, blackcurrants, redcurrants, half the raspberries and mint if using. Simmer for 5 minutes or till fruit softens but holds its shape still. Add remaining raspberries. Set aside.
3. Cut crusts off bread. Use slices to line a 1.2 litre/2 pint pudding bowl. Put first slice in the base then cut or tear the rest to line the sides. Don't leave gaps or the fruit leaks. Overlap a bit if you want. Neatness doesn't matter.
4. Spoon fruit into the lining. Include some juices to soak through and flavour the bread. Save excess juice for turning out time.
5. Seal the pud by covering the top with as much bread as you need.

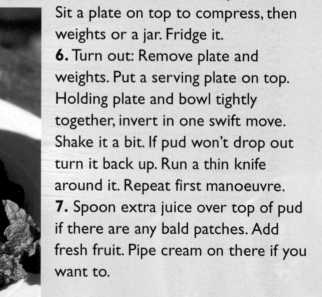

Sit a plate on top to compress, then weights or a jar. Fridge it.
6. Turn out: Remove plate and weights. Put a serving plate on top. Holding plate and bowl tightly together, invert in one swift move. Shake it a bit. If pud won't drop out turn it back up. Run a thin knife around it. Repeat first manoeuvre.
7. Spoon extra juice over top of pud if there are any bald patches. Add fresh fruit. Pipe cream on there if you want to.

Raspberry Ripple Fool

Got some soil? Grow some raspberry canes. For my money, a fresh raspberry is the best of summer fruit and works brilliantly in this creamy pud. It's got a homestyle raspberry sauce plus mashed berries. Stick in a bowl to eat on the sofa, or in a glass to make the most of it. Enjoy with a crisp biscuit.

For 3–4
450 g/1 lb fresh raspberries
2 tbsps caster sugar or more to taste
1–2 tsps rosewater
425 ml/³/4 pint double or whipping cream

Method

1. Put half the raspberries into a pan with half the sugar, rosewater and a splash of water. Simmer very gently until they start to release juice.

2. Sit a sieve over a bowl. Push contents of the pan through with a wooden spoon. Leave raspberry syrup to cool.

3. Whisk cream up with the rest of the sugar till soft and pillowy (not too stiff or grainy).

4. Mash remaining raspberries with a fork. Fold into the cream.

5. Either: Stir raspberry syrup gently into cream for a ripple effect. Slap into a dish or glasses. **Or:** Layer raspberry cream and syrup in glasses. Chill.

variation

SPEEDY FOOL
Whip cream and sugar. Mash in ripe mango, blackberries, blueberries, strawberries or lightly poached rhubarb.
CRUNCHY FOOL
Crumble in meringue, amaretti or ginger biscuit.

Golden Syrup Steamed Winter Pudding

The classic English old-school pudding. Everyone loves it. It's rich, moreish and warming. OK, it's a bit of a challenge, but that's what cooking's got to be about. For a lovely soft sponge and hot, sweet syrup sauce? Hey, it's got to be worth it. Make custard!

Method

1. Fill a steamer ⅓ full of water. Or fill a large saucepan with water to come ⅓ way up the sides of a 850 ml/1½ pint pudding basin (or a 1.2 litre/2 pint job for a saucier pudding). Put on the hob. Bring to a simmer.
2. Grease the inside of the pudding basin well with extra butter.
3. Spoon the golden syrup, juice and half the rind into a small heavy bottomed pan. Melt gently and stir to amalgamate.
4. Tip the breadcrumbs into the syrup mix. Pour into the basin.
5. Now, slap the butter and sugar into a large warm bowl. Use a wooden spoon to beat the two together till pale and light in texture.
6. Tip a little beaten egg into this mix while still beating. Continue bit by bit till it's all in. If the mix starts to separate add a pinch of flour and don't worry. If the bowl and ingredients are warm it shouldn't happen.
7. Sift the flour into the creamed mix. Add the rind of the second orange or the lemon. Using a large metal spoon and large scooping movements fold the dry ingredients into the mix together with 1 tablespoon water. You want the mix to be soft enough to drop off the end of the spoon. Add a bit more water if you need it.
8. Scoop and pour the mix on top of the syrup in the basin. It will look weird but that's OK.
9. Cut out a piece of foil that will more than cover the top of the basin. Grease one side then make a 5 cm/2 in fold across the middle so it can expand when the pud rises. Place the foil buttered side down over the top. Fold it down then tie round tightly with string (get someone to help). Trim off most excess foil but leaving a fringe to it.
10. Put the basin into your steamer or pan of simmering water. Steam for 1½ hours. Check and top up water levels every 10 minutes or so.
11. Remove pud. Cut string to release and remove the foil. Run a knife between the basin and pud to help release it. Place a large plate over the top. Quickly and carefully invert the plate. The boiling syrup sauce will flood out. Shake the bowl gently to release the pudding.

For 4
Butter for greasing
3 tbsps golden syrup
Juice of 2 oranges (or 1 orange and 1 lemon)
Rind of 2 oranges (or 1 orange and 1 lemon)
2 tbsps fresh white breadcrumbs
110 g/4 oz soft butter
110 g/4 oz caster sugar
2 eggs (beaten)
110 g/4 oz self-raising flour
1–2 tbsps cold water
String for pudding

Eat with:
Vanilla ice-cream (pg 117)
Crème fraîche

Custard
275 ml/10 fl oz milk
1 split vanilla pod, a few drops vanilla essence or a strip of lemon peel
3 eggs, separated
10 g/½ oz sugar
5 g/¼ oz cornflour

Heat the milk in a medium saucepan with vanilla pod, essence or lemon peel. Remove when it just boils (don't let it boil over). Take pod out if using. Slap egg yolks in a large bowl with sugar and cornflour. Mix well. Tip hot milk slowly onto mix while stirring with a wooden spoon. Tip back in the pan. Stir over a low heat till thickish. Don't boil – it'll curdle. Stir like mad with the pan in cold water if it gets grainy. Pour into a jug. Eat hot, cold or warm.

4 Styley Ice-creams

For 4
3–4 unwaxed lemons, washed and dried
175 g/6 oz icing sugar
200 ml/7 fl oz double cream
250 ml/9 fl oz Greek yogurt
3 tbsps very cold water

Eat with:
Cakes
Fruit salads
Sundaes

As you get older, good old Mr Whippy doesn't quite do it any more. Really you want something different and lighter. These four styley ices are so easy and don't require any fancy equipment. Perfect for summer. Brilliant for parties…

Tangy Lemon Yogurt Ice

Could an ice-cream get cooler? I don't think so…

Method
1. Grate lemons and squeeze out all their juice. Mix in a large bowl.
2. Sift sugar in through a sieve. Stir to amalgamate. Rest for 30 minutes.
3. Tip the cream, yogurt and water into another bowl. Whip together with a balloon whisk until just thick, not too stiff. Mix this gently into the lemon syrup with a metal spoon.
4. Pour ice-cream into a freezer container or free-standing freezer bag. Freeze. Get it out 10 minutes before you need it.

For 4
Juice of 6 large oranges
A good squeeze of lemon or lime juice

Orange Granita

A proper orange water ice … so good … totally refreshing.

Method
1. Mix the orange juice and lemon or lime juice.
2. Pour it into a freezer bag or box. Sit it in the freezer.
3. Every 20–30 minutes take it out. Break the ice up with a fork or whisk it.
4. Put it back in the freezer. Repeat a further 4 times. Lasts 3 weeks.

Strawberry Sorbet

Homestyle strawberry slushie… Go pick your own fruit when strawberries are rampant. Cooling for Verity after tennis.

Method

1. Tip the sugar and water into a heavy based pan. Dissolve the sugar over a low heat.

2. Increase and boil steadily for 5 minutes. Pour the syrup into a bowl. Add the lemon juice. Leave to get cold.

3. Mash the strawberries into a liquid using a fork. Or blitz in a liquidizer. Add the syrup and blitz them together.

4. Pour the liquid sorbet into a free-standing freezer bag or container. Sit it in the freezer until it starts to solidify. This could be 30 minutes or much longer depending on your freezer.

5. At this stage whisk the egg white. Take the sorbet out of the freezer and fold the egg white in to lift the mixture. Slap it back in the freezer.

For 4
175 g/6 oz caster sugar
570 ml/1 pint water
Juice of 1/2 lemon
350 g/12 oz strawberries
1 egg white

Coconut Ice-cream & Lime Syrup

Great tastes, great team … particularly soothing after curry or chilli. The syrup works well on most fruit salads…

Method

1. Ice-cream: To make by hand, tip the nut milk into a bowl with the sugar and whisk together. If using a blender, whisk the two together.

2. Pour the cream into a freezer bag or box. Slap it into the freezer.

3. Remove after 30 minutes. Break the mix up with a fork to reduce the ice crystals. Put it back in the freezer. Repeat.

4. When the ice-cream starts to solidify, whisk the egg white till stiff. Fold it into the mix. Freeze again.

5. Lime syrup: Tip water and sugar into a heavy based pan over gentle heat. Stir with a wooden spoon to dissolve. Increase heat. Boil for 2 minutes.

6. Tip into a bowl. Cool. Add finely grated zest and juice of limes. Chill.

7. Drizzle over ice-cream.

For 4
Ice-cream
400 ml/3/4 pint coconut
    milk
75 g/3 oz caster sugar
1 egg white

Lime syrup
125 ml/4 fl oz water
110 g/4 oz caster sugar
2–3 limes

Eat with:
Banana filled crêpes
Chocolate sauce
Banana sundae

Essential Extras

Real cooks get cooking essential extras.
So make 'em.

Shortcrust Pastry

The real thing handmade or processed. Sort it for all your pastry needs. Work fast with a light touch. You don't want concrete.

For 23 cm/9 in flan tin or 4 small tart tins
225 g/8 oz plain or white flour
Pinch of salt
110 g/4 oz cold butter (use soft butter for processor method)
2–3 tbsps very cold water

Hand method
1. Sift the flour and salt into a large bowl. Cut butter small.
2. Add butter to flour. Rub in lightly with your fingers till it looks like breadcrumbs.
3. Add 2 tbsps cold water. Mix with a fork till the pastry starts to form. Bring dough together quickly with your fingers. Handle very lightly. Add the remaining water if needed.
4. Wrap in clingfilm and leave for 20 minutes to chill. Bring back to room temperature before using.

Processor method
1. Tip flour and salt into a processor.
2. Add butter. Process till mixed.
3. Add half the water. Process. Add the rest gradually (may not need it all) until pastry is soft and pliable, not sticky.
4. Remove on to a lightly floured board and use for recipe.

STOCKS

I freeze a lotta stock. Makes great soups, risotto, gravy, casseroles and sauces.

Chicken Stock

1 roast chicken carcass
2 onions, quartered
1 celery stick, cut into chunks
1 carrot, cut into chunks
Garlic cloves, peeled
1 leek, cut into chunks (optional)
A few fresh herb sprigs, tied with cotton (optional)
3.4 litres/6 pints water

Method
1. Chuck chicken carcass with any jelly, gravy and meat into a large saucepan. Add the onions, celery, carrot, garlic, leek and herbs (if using).
2. Pour in the water to cover. The pan should not be too full.
3. Bring to a boil. Skim off any scum. Simmer on a low heat for 2–3 hours.
4. Strain stock through a colander over a large bowl. Cool. Cover with clingfilm. Chill or freeze.

Vegetable Stock

2 large onions
1 celery stick
2 leeks
3 carrots
Few black peppercorns
Fresh parsley sprigs
2.3 litres/4 pints water
Juice of 1 lemon
2 garlic cloves
2 tsps salt

Method
1. Wash and roughly chop all the veg. Chuck in a large saucepan with all the other ingredients.
2. Bring to the boil. Half cover. Simmer for 1–2 hours. Strain through a fine sieve.

DIPS, SAUCES & SPREADS

Easy Raspberry Jam

What it says on the jar. Easy. Jam. Only takes 20 minutes.

Makes 3 x 200 ml/7 fl oz jars or 6 small jars of jam
450 g/1 lb raspberries (fresh or defrosted)
450 g/1 lb jam sugar

Method
1. Sit your jars on a baking tray in a warm oven (140°C/275°F/gas 1).
2. Put a saucer in the fridge to chill.
3. Tip rinsed raspberries into a large, heavy-bottomed pan. Cook gently for 2–3 minutes, stirring with a wooden spoon.
4. When the juices flow add the jam sugar. Stir till it dissolves.
5. Whack up the heat and boil furiously for 5 minutes.
6. Do the set test. Get the saucer from the fridge. Spoon a tiny bit of jam on to it. Leave for 1 minute then push the jam with a finger. If it wrinkles up then it is ready. If not boil for a further 2 minutes then test again. Repeat till wrinkly.
7. Leave jam off the heat to settle for 5 minutes while you remove the warmed jars. Using a small ladle or large spoon very carefully fill each jar almost to the top. Take care, it will be so hot.
8. Top each pot with a disc of waxed paper, wax side down. Then a transparent cover or lid. Wipe the jars down. Label and date when cool. Delicious.

Apple Sauce

Pork wouldn't be the same without it … nor would bangers, crêpes, anything that needs apple sauce.

2 apples, peeled, cored and chopped
Blob of butter

Sugar
Squeeze of lemon juice
Ground cinnamon (optional)

Method
1. Slap the apples in a pan with a bit of water and butter.
2. Cook very gently, stirring till the fruit gets mushy, adding more liquid if you need. Beat for a smooth sauce.
3. Taste and flavour with a bit of sugar and lemon juice and a pinch of ground cinnamon if you like it.

Apple Chutney
Makes 4 x 900 g/2 lb jars

2 kg/4$^{1}/_{2}$ lb cooking apples, peeled, cored and chopped
4 cloves garlic, crushed
600 ml/1 pint malt vinegar
700 g/1$^{1}/_{2}$ lb soft dark brown sugar
125 g/4$^{1}/_{2}$ oz stoned dates, chopped
3 tsps ground ginger
1 tsp ground mixed spice
Large pinch of cayenne pepper
1 tsp salt

Method
1. Tip the apples, garlic and half the vinegar into a large heavy-based saucepan.
2. Cook gently, stirring regularly with a wooden spoon till thick.
3. Add the remaining vinegar, sugar, dates, ginger, spices and salt. Cook for 30 minutes, stirring, till thick and sludgy with the odd lump of fruit.
4. Wash jars well. Dry and place on a baking tray. Warm in the oven at 140°C/275°F/gas 1.
5. Ladle chutney into the jars. Put a wax disc from a jam kit directly on to the chutney. Dampen a cellophane disc to cover each pot. Secure with an elastic band.
6. Wipe jars while warm. Label when cold. Leave for 2 months before eating.

Homestyle Mayo
2 egg yolks
$^{1}/_{2}$ tsp each of salt, dry mustard and caster sugar
250 ml/8 fl oz sunflower or groundnut oil
50 ml/2 fl oz olive oil
2 tbsps white wine vinegar or lemon juice
1 tbsp hot water

Method
1. Chuck the egg yolks into a bowl. Add salt, mustard and sugar. Beat till smooth with a balloon whisk. Sit the bowl on a tea towel to stop it slipping.
2. Mix the oils in a jug. Pour half the oil, drip by drip, on to the egg mix, whisking all the time. Keep it slow to start, so the mix won't curdle. After a bit it'll start to thicken. Stir in 1 tbsp vinegar or lemon juice.
3. Pour in remaining oil in a slow trickle. Keep whisking. Add water and remaining vinegar or lemon.
4. Taste. Adjust seasoning. Keeps for a week in an airtight container in the fridge.

variations
At STEP 1, add for:
GARLIC MAYO (AIOLI)
2 crushed garlic cloves.
MUSTARD & DILL MAYO
2 tsps sugar and 2 tbsps Dijon mustard. Then use 150 ml/5 fl oz sunflower oil (no olive oil) and 1 tbsp white wine vinegar. When mixed, stir in 1–2 tbsps fresh chopped dill.
HARISSA MAYO
2 tbsps harissa paste instead of mustard.

Homestyle Ketchup
Easy to make and healthy.

500 g/18 oz ripe tomatoes, quartered (with stalks and stems attached)
2 cloves garlic, crushed
50 g/2 oz brown sugar
60 ml/2$^{1}/_{2}$ fl oz cider or white wine vinegar
Good pinch of mustard powder
4 shakes of Worcester sauce
Salt and pepper

Method
1. Slap ingredients into a large pan. Put on a medium–high heat and bring to the boil. Reduce at once. Simmer very gently for 45–60 mins, or till the mix is sludgy with very little liquid.
2. Pull out any stems or stalks with a fork. Blitz the mix in a processor or blender.
3. Pour through a sieve. Cool, then store in a sterilized jar (washed then heated. Seal well once filled), or cover. Store in the fridge for a fortnight.

variation
At STEP 2 add one medium onion, quartered, and/or fresh chilli.

Tomato Salsa
4 ripe tomatoes, finely chopped
1 fresh red or green chilli, de-seeded and finely chopped
2 shallots or 1 small onion, finely chopped
2 tbsps fresh coriander, chopped
1 lime
Pinch of caster sugar
Salt and black pepper

Method
1. Mix the tomatoes, chilli, shallots or onion, and coriander.
2. Mix in a good squeeze or two of lime juice, sugar, salt and pepper.

Homestyle Pesto
110 g/4 oz fresh basil, coriander or rocket leaves
150 ml/5 fl oz olive oil
25 g/1 oz pine nuts

2 large cloves garlic, peeled
50 g/2 oz Parmesan, grated

Method
1. Blitz basil, coriander or rocket, olive oil, pine nuts and garlic in a food processor.
2. Tip into a bowl. Mix in Parmesan. Cover. Chill.

Tzatziki

Half a cucumber, peeled and finely chopped
2 cloves garlic, crushed
300 ml/½ pint Greek-style yogurt
Salt and pepper

Method
1. Mix the cucumber and garlic into the yogurt.
2. Season.

Guacamole

2 shallots or 1 small onion, chopped
1 clove garlic, crushed
2 ripe avocados (Hass are good)
Juice of 1 lemon or lime
Pinch of cayenne pepper
Pinch of salt
1 tbsp fresh coriander leaves, chopped (optional)

Method
1. Blitz the shallots or onion and garlic in a processor.
2. Add the avocado flesh, lemon or lime juice, cayenne and salt. Blitz again, with coriander if using.
3. Tip the guacamole in a bowl. Eat before it browns.

Hummus

400 g/14 oz can chickpeas, drained
2 cloves garlic, crushed
1 tbsp tahini
Juice of 1 lemon
Pinch of salt
2 tbsps olive oil
2 tbsps water
Paprika (optional)
Fresh coriander, chopped (optional)
Few pine nuts (optional)

Method
1. Tip the chickpeas into a processor. Add garlic, tahini, lemon juice and salt.
2. Heat (don't boil) olive oil and water in a small saucepan.
3. Add the liquid to the processor. Blitz till smooth. Add more water or lemon if the mix is too firm and blitz again.
4. Taste and season. Sprinkle with paprika, coriander and/or pine nuts.
5. Eat warm, or drizzle with olive oil and chill.

DRESSINGS & SALADS

My Sparky Dressing

Good pinch of sugar
Pinch of salt
1 tbsp balsamic vinegar
4–6 tbsps extra virgin olive oil

Method
1. **Either:** Whisk the sugar, salt and vinegar together in a bowl. Add the olive oil bit by bit. **Or:** Stick the lot in a jar, put the lid on and shake it.
2. Taste, and adjust flavours.

Honey & Mustard

2 tsps wholegrain mustard
1 tsp honey
1 clove garlic, crushed
2 tbsps lemon juice or white wine vinegar
Salt and black pepper
6 tbsps olive oil

Method
1. Tip all the ingredients except oil into a jar. Close and shake.
2. Add the oil and shake again.

Classic Green Salad

Any green leaves (e.g. rocket, little gem, English salad lettuce, watercress, lamb's lettuce, baby spinach, cos, chopped chicory)

Method
1. Mix any of these.
2. Toss in a simple olive oil dressing or something creamy.

Tomato Salad

2 or 3 ripe tomatoes
A little salt and pepper
Pinch of caster sugar
Dressing
1 tsp caster sugar
1 tsp English or Dijon mustard
Salt and pepper
2 tbsps wine vinegar (red, white, cider, sherry)
6 tbsps olive oil
1 clove garlic, crushed (optional)

Method
1. Slice the tomatoes into 1 cm/⅓ in thick slices. Lay them on a plate in a single layer. Sprinkle with the salt, pepper and sugar.
2. Whisk dressing ingredients together. Drizzle over tomatoes immediately to max the flavour.
3. Toss the tomatoes gently in the dressing.

variation

TOMATO & ONION SALAD
Chuck finely chopped shallot or thinly sliced red onion over dressed salad.

Classic Orange Salad

So refreshing.

Green leaves: spinach, rocket, watercress or chopped chicory
2 oranges, peeled, sliced and cut in segments (save juice)
2 carrots, grated
6 fresh dates or dried ones, chopped
Honey & Mustard dressing

Method
1. Slap leaves on two plates or bowls.
2. Top with orange segments, carrots and dates.
3. Toss with my dressing, plus juice from the oranges.

variation

Add cashew nuts or poppy seeds.

Orange & Pomegranate

2 oranges, peeled and sliced
Pomegranate molasses

Method

Slap the oranges on a plate with a drizzle of pomegranate molasses for dipping. Fizzy.

Coleslaw

110 g/4 oz white cabbage, shredded
1 large carrot, grated
1½ tbsps mayo (pg 139)
1 tsp mustard
Drizzle of honey
Handful of raisins or dates
Salt and black pepper

Method

1. Stick the cabbage and carrot in a bowl.
2. Mix the other stuff.
3. Slap it over and mix well.

Roast Pepper Salad

4 red or orange peppers
3 tbsps olive oil
Salt and pepper

Method

1. Preheat oven to 230°C/450°F/ gas 8.
2. Sit peppers on a baking tray. Cook for 30 mins till blistered, turning once.
3. Sit them in a freezer bag for 15 minutes then peel and de-seed.
4. Cut into strips. Drizzle with olive oil and season.

Courgette Ribbon Salad

2 courgettes
2 tbsps olive oil
1 tbsp balsamic vinegar
1 clove garlic, crushed
Pinch of sugar
Salt and pepper

Method

1. Cut ends off courgettes. Slicing lengthways with a mandolin or spud peeler, make ribbons of very thin courgette.
2. Whisk up the remaining ingredients. Tip over the ribbons.

Index

Index

Cheers to Jess Taylor, Henry Preen, Ariyo Onafowokan, Joe Coulter, Andy Walkland, Olivia Towers, Verity Miers and Dom Hanley for challenging me and being such great mates.

To York University, York City Football Club and Next Generation Gym for the use of their sports facilities; Imp-Hut Ltd for use of their recording studio; City Screen Ltd; and The Farmers Cart, Towthorpe.

To Louise Rooke (champion food taster and washer-up!)
To dad for being dad
To Stevie G for all the time off!
Thanks to Lorne and the Walker people
Thanks to all my lovely family

www.walkerbooks.co.uk
www.samstern.co.uk

First published 2007 by Walker Books Ltd
87 Vauxhall Walk, London SE11 5HJ

10 9 8 7 6 5 4 3 2 1

© 2007 Sam and Susan Stern

Photography by Lorne Campbell. Susan Stern photograph by Jeffrey Stern

The right of Sam Stern and Susan Stern to be identified as authors of this work has been asserted by them in accordance with the Copyright, Designs and Patents Act 1988

This book has been typeset in GillSans

Printed in Italy

British Library Cataloguing in Publication Data: a catalogue record for this book is available from the British Library

ISBN 978-1-4063-0560-9